**Equity and Efficiency Effects
from Manpower Programs**

Equity and Efficiency Effects from Manpower Programs

Corry F. Azzi
Lawrence University

Lexington Books
D.C. Heath and Company
Lexington, Massachusetts
Toronto   London

331.11
A999e

Library of Congress Cataloging in Publication Data

Azzi, Corry F.
  Equity and efficiency effects from manpower programs.

  Includes bibliographical references.
  1. Manpower policy—United States. 2. Human capital.
3. Cost effectiveness. I. Title.
HD5724.A98   331.1'1'0973   72-7022
ISBN 0-669-85084-5

Published simultaneously in Canada.

74-4/5 76

Printed in the United States of America.

International Standard Book Number: 0-669-85084-5

Library of Congress Catalog Card Number: 72-7022

Contents

List of Figures

List of Tables

x

Acknowledgments

I am indebted to James Cox, Peter Doeringer, John Dunlop, Ronald Ehrenberg, and Marc Roberts for their comments on earlier drafts. I have been the beneficiary of considerable research assistance from Connie Brown and Susan Greenbaughm. Morla Tjossem edited the manuscript. Since much of the research was done while I was a graduate student, I acknowledge the "financial assistance" of my wife.

Introduction

Although the recent development and proliferation of federally subsidized manpower programs designed to benefit the disadvantaged has received considerable attention, studies which have attempted to quantify the costs and benefits of these programs have been inadequate.[1] By assuming that wages equal marginal value product, the analyses have been based on highly unrealistic models of the behavior of firms. Consequently, such studies may not have provided accurate information on both the magnitude and distribution of program costs and benefits.

Manpower programs may be established to achieve several objectives. Along with provision of income benefits for the disadvantaged, objectives could be: improvement in matching people with job vacancies they can adequately fill, increase in the labor productivity, and elimination of labor market bottlenecks that inhibit economic growth. Benefits for the disadvantaged need not be the only justification for programs with enrollees who have had difficulty finding high wage employment. Increasing economic efficiency, measured as the sum of dollar benefits in excess of costs, may be a justification for manpower programs that add to laborers' skills and improve labor resource allocations. Benefits from increased economic efficiency may accrue to consumers and corporate shareholders as well as to the disadvantaged. Whatever the objectives of a manpower program, both the magnitude and distribution of costs and benefits will vary with the content of training, the amount of funds expended per trainee, and the socioeconomic characteristics of the trainees. This study considers only the direct economic effects of some typical programs offering the disadvantaged training in vocational skills.

The Way Manpower Programs
Implement Their Objectives

Whatever the complex objectives that led to the funding of programs for the disadvantaged, to be successful these programs must induce training and employment opportunities not being generated by market forces. Such opportunities should create income for the disadvantaged. Because job opportunities can be induced in a number of ways, we find considerable variation among manpower programs. For example, JOBS programs offer direct payments to firms to cover at least some cost of recruitment, screening, and on-the-job training. Other training programs are external to firms. These institutional out-of-plant programs, from storefronts to vocational high schools, may be divided into two broad categories, those which train for skills such as welding or automobile repair and those which develop verbal or mathematical abilities.

Both institutional programs and some on-the-job programs may also offer counseling. Still other programs, instead of training, provide already screened job applicants to firms. Finally, some programs upgrade definable groups within a firm's existing labor force. These programs work to gain promotions for persons who ordinarily could not be promoted within a plant and are locked into dead end jobs.[2] The considerable differences among programs intended to serve a common general purpose are more apparent than real, because all programs may alter market-induced job and training opportunities by subsidizing firms.

That on-the-job training programs embody a subsidy payment to firms should be self-evident. These programs by offering direct payments to firms presumably induce activities that they would not undertake without such payments. Out-of-plant training, screening, and counseling programs can be as much a subsidy to firms as the on-the-job programs. The only exception may be an out-of-plant program that teaches completely general skills in a perfectly competitive labor market. But labor markets are not perfectly competitive; and even if they were, to the extent that such programs also provide screening and counseling they are in fact providing services that otherwise would have to be purchased by the firms. Whether programs are on the job or out of plant, all allocate public funds, some of which may be used by firms either directly or indirectly to lower their costs. This would alter the preferences of those firms and could affect hiring or promotion decisions.

Because these programs may subsidize employers in their attempt to aid employees, we are led to a crucial question: to what extent are the benefits of these subsidy programs generally retained by employers instead of being passed on to employees? Employees would be the primary beneficiaries if we assume that wages equal marginal value product, but that assumption excludes the existence of specific skills and institutions such as unions and does not admit the importance of work rules and patterns of social interaction that become, over time, normative standards for behavior within a plant. These rules and traditional patterns affect wage rates, hiring decisions, and work assignments and tend to be rigid in the short run.[3] Since perfectly competitive market forces do not in themselves determine the allocation of labor, and labor is not vested with only general skills, a model designed to measure the magnitude and distribution of program benefits should not assume that wages equal marginal value product.

Distribution of Costs and Benefits

Employers and employees who benefit from manpower programs are from diverse socioeconomic groups. If we value an even distribution of consumption, then the distribution of program benefits across these groups is relevant to our evaluation of the social desirability of these programs. The distribution of program costs among taxpayers is also relevant because available data on the distributions of stock ownership and tax burdens indicates that benefits for employers represent a regressive redistribution from taxpayers to relatively wealthier corporate stockholders.[4] The importance of the distribution of costs does not depend upon the assumption that the programs embody a marginal change in tax liabilities. In fact, this study assumes that the funds required for the programs are drawn from the federal tax pool created by personal income, corporate and federal excise and inheritance taxes, and that tax rates are unaffected by manpower programs. Whether or not tax liabilities are affected, determining if a federal project or program is to be funded should be dependent on the socioeconomic status of federal taxpayers. For example, if federal taxes fall completely on corporate shareholders, then we might favor a manpower program that distributed only a small proportion of its benefits to the poor and a large portion to shareholders, because on net the program would have a desirable distributional impact. On the other hand, we might judge the same expenditure program undesirable if federal taxes were paid by the poor. Even though an expenditure program does not embody a marginal change in tax liabilities, the question of who pays taxes and therefore who sacrifices the consumption required to finance the program is still relevant to program evaluation.

If public sector expenditures are constrained, then manpower programs impose an additional cost because other feasible public expenditure programs and projects are displaced. This cost is the net benefits that these programs would have generated. Available data do suggest that benefits from federal expenditures increase as a proportion of income as income decreases.[5] But if manpower programs distribute part of their benefits to shareholders, not only is the redistribution from taxpayers to shareholders regressive, but if public sector expenditure is constrained, the manpower programs are displacing other federal expenditures that on average have socially desirable distributional impacts. This does not mean that a manpower program that benefits shareholders is necessarily undesirable, but a judgment about the merit of the program should include information about any regressive redistribution.

Since manpower programs exist in an uncertain world bounded by institutional constraints such as work rules and traditions, where information is not complete or perfect, and where employees are vested with specific skills, the analyses of manpower programs will be based on a human capital model where marginal value product need not equal wages.

The Model

The model relates investment in human capital to the behavior of firms and will be used first to discuss the hiring and training decisions, assuming fixed wages and prices of training resources. It emphasizes the importance of training costs and job performance as measured by absenteeism, turnover, and productivity. Differences in expected training costs and job performances among a diverse group of job applicants will be demonstrated to be important to hiring, training, and promotion decisions if wages are fixed and not necessarily equal to marginal value product. If this situation exists, marginal value produce in excess of wages is a return to the firm which it can affect by selecting employees who require minimal training expenditures and offer relatively good job performance.

If manpower programs are to provide consumption benefits for the disadvantaged, hiring, training, and promoting such persons must be made more profitable for firms. This may be accomplished by reducing the private costs of training them to surpass minimum standards of performance required for any job. But reducing the private training costs and increasing the training of any disadvantaged person does not necessarily mean that the beneficiaries of the manpower programs will be those trained under federal subsidies. To the extent that the subsidy programs do not alter hiring or promotion decisions, firms benefit from better trained employees and reduced training costs.

The model is used to identify two sets of conditions. Under the first the subsidy program would distribute a significant proportion of benefits to the disadvantaged. Under the second, it would distribute significant benefits to the firm and shareholders, with minimal or zero benefits to the disadvantaged. Given the two sets, one may infer which would be more often duplicated in the real world. In fact, the model suggests the hypothesis that many manpower programs benefit mostly firms and shareholders, and benefits for the disadvantaged may not offset the costs imposed on taxpayers. This hypothesis will be tested in the empirical study of two firms that have contracted for manpower programs.

Empirical Study

The purpose of the empirical study is to see if the training programs have altered the two establishments' hiring and promotion decisions in favor of the trainees. Several significant users of manpower program labor in one urban center were approached. The two firms surveyed agreed to cooperate in a detailed in-plant study in order to get information about their costs and benefits from manpower programs. This study used the estimates of the establishments' costs and benefits as significant factors in judging the distributions and magnitudes of the programs' net benefits.

The two establishments are similar to the extent that both are part of national multi-plant enterprises. Their plants are, however, very different. One builds ships. It employs several thousand workers in a unionized plant with undesirable working conditions. The skills it uses—welding, shipfitting, pipefitting, and sheetmetal work—are craft skills that are demanded by companies in the construction industry. Because the skills are used by many other companies, a significant proportion of the firm's applicants typically indicate experience with required skills. The other firm mass produces light electronic components for computers. It has a non-unionized plant that is clean, air-conditioned, and well-lighted. Its applicants rarely have previous experience in the skills that it uses. Differences between the firms in their attitudes about training and wage assignment practices reflect their differences in the frequency of finding job applicants with the required skills. The electronic components manufacturer views training as one of its normal business activities in contrast to the shipbuilder's attitude that training of unskilled hires is a burden created by the scarcity of skilled job applicants. Although both firms pay hourly wages, an employee's wage with the components manufacturer is determined by his production department and job title. For the skills surveyed in the study a new employee's assignment to a job and department is not noticeably sensitive to his previous employment. In contrast a starting job and wage with the shipbuilder is a function of the skills he developed on his previous jobs. Generally the shipbuilder assigns different jobs to persons whose proficiency in the same skill differs, although it can be observed paying different hourly rates to persons differing in proficiency but performing the same jobs.

The impact of the manpower programs on hiring decisions can be determined by identifying comparison groups hired without subsidies into the same entry port jobs as trainees. The non-subsidized groups are chosen by taking random samples of the firm's personnel files. The socioeconomic variables used to compare the subsidized and non-subsidized groups are those listed on the application forms in the personnel files. This data is used under the assumption that if a firm bothered to collect the information, it was relevant to their hiring decisions. If the normal source of labor inputs is socioeconomically identical to trainees, then one is confronted with strong evidence that the subsidy programs have not created new job opportunities for the trainees.

Even if the programs do not alter hiring decisions, they may create benefits by either reducing training costs or improving job performance, which increases economic efficiency. The study will evaluate the impact of the programs on job performance as measured by absenteeism, turnover, and productivity. The firms provided information on these cost parameters for each person in the sample. With this information we will estimate the benefits of reduced costs or improved performance which are retained by employers rather than passed on to the employees as higher wages and more frequent promotions.

The study is intended to determine whether the manpower programs have significantly benefited the disadvantaged or have benefited mostly the firms. It will illustrate how data often collected by firms as normal business practice can be used to provide more detailed information about the effects of manpower programs than has been made available by other studies. This information may contradict the conclusion typical in other studies that manpower programs for the disadvantaged have been socially desirable.

Notes

1. See Sar A. Levitan, "Manpower Aspects of the Economic Opportunity Act," INDUSTRIAL RELATIONS RESEARCH ASSOCIATION 21 (1968): 172-181; Garth Mangum, "Evaluating Federal Manpower Programs," INDUSTRIAL RELATIONS RESEARCH ASSOCIATION 21 (1968): 161-171; and U.S., Department of Labor, MANPOWER REPORT OF THE PRESIDENT (Washington, D.C.: Government Printing Office, March, 1970) for examples of rather optimistic evaluations of manpower programs. Earl D. Main, "A Nationwide Evaluation of MDTA Institutional Job Training," THE JOURNAL OF HUMAN RESOURCES 3 (May, 1968): 159-170, admits that, "The major unresolved question is how much of the estimated net effect of training on employment is really due to some other variable not included in the analysis." This criticism is general to manpower program studies.

2. Actually, these programs are very similar in their economic impacts to those programs that are primarily intended to affect hiring decisions. Thus, in subsequent theoretical discussions, when manpower programs are referred to as subsidies that affect hiring decisions, we could substitute promotion decisions for hiring decisions without revising the arguments.

3. Peter B. Doeringer and Michael J. Piore, INTERNAL LABOR MARKETS AND MANPOWER ANALYSIS (Lexington, Mass.: Heath Lexington Books, 1971), discuss the effect of rules and tradition on the allocation of labor.

4. Several studies on the distribution of the federal tax burden are available. See for example, G.A. Bishop, "The Tax Burden by Income Class," NATIONAL TAX JOURNAL 14 (March, 1961): 41-59; Richard A. Musgrave et al., "Distribution of Tax Payments by Income Groups: A Case Study for 1948," NATIONAL TAX JOURNAL 4 (March, 1951): 1-53; Joseph A. Pechman, FEDERAL TAX POLICY (Washington, D.C.: The Brookings Institute, 1966); and Rufus S. Turner, "Distribution of Tax Burdens in 1948," NATIONAL TAX JOURNAL 4 (Sept., 1951): 269-285. With the information and the following sources one has convincing evidence that transferring a dollar of federal tax receipts to shareholders represents a perverse redistribution. New York Stock Exchange, Board of Governors, FACT BOOK (New York: New York Stock Exchange, 1970), 5, 45, 47; U.S., Internal Revenue Service, STATISTICS OF INCOME 1967: INDIVIDUAL INCOME TAX RETURNS (Washington, D.C.: Government Printing Office, 1969), 34, 39, 41 (Tables 11, 13, and 14).

5. W. Irwin Gillespie, "Effect of Public Expenditures on the Distribution of Income," ESSAYS IN FISCAL FEDERALISM ed. by Richard A. Musgrave (Washington, D.C.: The Brookings Institute, 1965), 122-186; and Harold M. Hochman and James D. Rodgers, "Pareto Optimal Redistribution," AMERICAN ECONOMIC REVIEW 59 (Sept., 1969): 555.

**Equity and Efficiency Effects
from Manpower Programs**

1

Human Capital and Distributional Outputs from Manpower Programs

Before we can present empirical data on the distribution and magnitude of manpower program benefits, we must develop a model that relates market forces to the hiring and training decisions that firms make without such programs. This is crucial because the type of manpower programs analyzed in this book are those intended to affect the income and consumption of the disadvantaged. Whether such manpower programs provide general or specific training, whether that training occurs on the job or in an institutional setting, manpower programs generally accomplish their purpose by changing the cost to firms of inputs. This displaces the equilibrium that would have resulted if market forces had been left to operate without distortion.

The only exception when subsidized training would not displace the equilibrium of a firm is completely general training under the assumptions that resource markets are perfectly competitive and that subsidies cover only costs that a trainee would have paid. Gary Becker demonstrated that in a perfectly competitive resource market, the marginal employee would willingly pay all costs of general training until discounted costs equaled the discounted value of the incremental wage stream created by the training.[1] If the government subsidizes only costs that the employee would have willingly paid, then his discounted earning stream increases because his costs of training have been reduced. The employer's equilibrium would not be affected. If the government subsidizes general training that neither the employee nor the employer would have purchased, then given perfect competition the employee can demand wages that are higher than those he would have received without subsidized training. This would displace the employer's equilibrium.

Becker required the assumption of perfect competition to develop a sharp distinction between the effects of general and specific training. The model presented in this chapter is based on more reasonable assumptions about labor markets. In this model the distinction between general and specific training fades, because subsidizing either will have similar, although not identical, effects on the hiring, training, wage, and output decisions of firms.

This chapter will concentrate on the impact of a program for the disadvantaged on a firm that has consented to employ subsidized laborers. Attention will be centered on the potential of such a program to alter the hiring, training, internal allocation of labor, and wage payment decisions of a firm, because these decisions must be affected if a manpower program is to aid those persons who are intended to benefit. With the model, we will be able to ask the

1

crucial question: is it reasonable to expect that manpower programs have altered these decisions in a manner that generates significant benefits for the disadvantaged?

Simply because a program distributes some share of the value of its outputs to shareholders does not necessarily imply that the program should not be instituted. But an administrator may be faced with some very difficult choices when deciding whether to fund a program. One may imagine an administrator required to approve or disapprove each element in a set of feasible manpower programs. If he has adequate information, he may develop a reasonable set of expectations about the magnitude and distribution of the value of outputs from each. Some programs may benefit trainees substantially in excess of input costs imposed on taxpayers. Other programs may offer outputs that are less than input costs and are distributed mostly to shareholders. Decisions about such programs may not be difficult. But the administrator may face more difficult choices.

If intelligent and sometimes difficult choices are to be made, then information about the distribution and magnitude of program outputs must be gathered. Available information is inadequate. The theoretical discussion therefore serves two purposes. First, it yields insights into the possible distributional as well as efficiency impacts of such programs. In effect, the theoretical discussion will suggest hypotheses for testing. Second, the theory dictates what kinds of data are necessary for an adequate investigation of these hypotheses. This chapter will discuss both the hypotheses suggested by the theory and the data needed to test these hypotheses.

Human Capital and the Theory of the Firm

This presentation assumes that simple neoclassical wage theory does not isolate all relevant costs. If in all time periods a firm hires until marginal value product equals a market determined wage rate, then firms would incur no cost due to turnover. Firms would not choose to train their employees since training costs would not be covered by income in excess of wage costs. Traditional wage theory cannot explain the preference of firms for stable, reliable employees capable of offering substantial increments to productivity per unit of training cost.

The investment approach to human capital is consequently a better analytical technique. It states that at any time zero a firm would select a hiring and training policy to maximize the sum of net present discounted values earned from its employees. The net present discounted value, $NPDV_i$, earned from the ith employee is a function of his incremental contribution to the discounted value of the firm's output over time minus initial period costs of recruiting and screening him and the discounted value of his wage and training costs. The firm would continue to hire employees at time zero until $NPDV_m = 0$, where m denotes the marginal employee.

The human capital model emphasizes cost parameters that cannot be considered in simple wage theory. The most important of these is training costs. Such costs are often most substantial in the first few periods of a worker's employment. The theory considers not only the magnitude but also emphasizes the timing of such costs. The human capital approach is similar to the theory of fixed capital in that it typically assumes that an investor makes purchases in the present and near future in order to earn returns in the more distant future. Unlike the theory of fixed capital, human capital is invested in an autonomous agent who is capable of limiting the firm's return stream simply by terminating his employment. Thus the firm's expectations as to the future actions of its prospective employees are crucial to its decisions both as to which persons it would choose to hire and to how much training it is prepared to invest in each employee. Training costs are essential in explaining a firm's preference for stable, reliable, long-term employees.

Logically, a firm would be concerned also with the ability of its employees to yield increments to productivity per dollar of training cost invested in them. Therefore the firm should prefer persons who can quickly and efficiently master their assigned tasks.

With preferences for these persons, the firm invests in recruitment and screening that are intended to attract adequate numbers of new employees who will perform up to the firm's standards. While its willingness to invest in screening and recruitment is certainly a function of the tightness of the labor market and of the quality of applicants the firm is currently receiving and expects to receive in the near future, these relationships have been discussed elsewhere and need not be pursued in detail here.[2] We need only assert the very general relationship: as the labor market tightens or the quality of the average applicant falls, the firm would be likely to increase its expenditures on recruitment, screening, and training.

Having discussed the general attributes of the human capital model, we can turn to measurable aspects of employees' job performances, such as turnover, absenteeism, and productivity. These react through both market and nonmarket forces to affect the returns to a firm and consequently to affect its hiring, training, internal labor allocation, and wage payments. The discussion will emphasize these measurable elements, because subsequent empirical studies will concentrate on them.

To begin with, assume that the job performance and costs of any new employee would be the same as those of any other chosen at random from a firm's applicant population. This unrealistic assumption simplifies the following discussion without affecting the conclusions. After the simpler analysis, equilibrium conditions will be discussed under the assumption that the firm faces a heterogeneous population of job applicants with identifiable subgroups offering distinctly different job performances. It will be argued that with wage differentials, the employment of some less productive and less reliable employees may represent the profit maximizing alternative for the firm. Although this is not a very surprising conclusion, it is crucial to the subsequent analysis of the impact of manpower programs.

Productivity

In the theory of human capital, the productivity of any employee, given fixed capital, is not exogenously determined but is a function of the training resources allocated by a firm to that employee. One may reasonably assume that an employee's marginal value product at any point in time, MVP_{it}, is a function of that laborer's skills when hired as well as improvement of them and the development of new ones. With MVP'_{it} defined to be the increment in marginal value product in time t and with the assumption that once a skill is learned it cannot be unlearned, any increment in productivity in t yields constant undiscounted returns to period T, when the employee terminates. MVP'_{it} is a function of the vector of training inputs, V_{it}, purchased for the ith employee in period t, and v^j_{it} is the jth element of that vector.

Of course, training can affect wages as well as productivity. But assuming for the moment perfectly competitive resource markets in a certain world with complete and perfect information, specific training does not benefit an employee by increasing his market value and he would not pay the cost of such training.[3] The firm would have to pay the cost and would purchase resource j for the training of person i in period t until

$$(1.1) \qquad \frac{\sum\limits_{s=t}^{T} \delta MVP'_{it}/(1+d)^s}{\delta v^j_{it}} = \frac{P_j}{(1+d)^t}$$

where p_j is the price of resource j and d is the relevant discount rate. Condition (1.1) is the first order condition for maximization of returns to the firm from specific training.

With perfectly competitive resource markets, the benefits of general training would accrue to employees as higher wages. Because the firm would have no inducement to provide such resources, the employee would have to pay for his own general training. Thus, $p_j v^j_{it}$ would represent cost to the employee. Condition (1.1) would be unaffected and is the first order condition for maximization of the employee's discounted wage stream.[4]

The productivity of any employee is a function of his skills when hired and vectors of training inputs. Condition (1.1) indicates that given initial skills, productivity at any point in time is determined by training resource prices and an employee's ability to yield productivity increments per unit of training resource input. With competitive markets this ability affects both wages and $NPDV_i$ because general training increases the market value of the employee while specific training generates a return stream in excess of wage payments.

Selection of a Training Program. For training procedure, the firm must choose between informal and formal programs. The responsibility for informal training is assigned to the experienced employees and is incidental to production and designated work. The cost of informal training is the loss in production caused by experienced employees dividing their efforts between production and training. Formal training uses experienced employees, operating materials, and capital equipment allocated to one task, initiating and maintaining the learning process. An alternative to formal training on the job where the trainee is expected to contribute to salable production, is formal out-of-plant or vestibule training, where an employee reaches a specified proficiency before he is assigned to the work place. Obviously, training expenditures and their allocation among program alternatives must be simultaneously determined where the optimal training program satisfied condition (1.1) and maximizes discounted returns in excess of discounted training costs.

Efficiency. Having outlined the conditions for an efficient allocation of resources for both general and specific training, we could inquire whether competitive market forces would lead to efficient training. Although an interesting theoretical development, it would be irrelevant to a discussion of manpower programs. In a world where labor and management spend considerable effort in establishing agreements that insulate them from competitive resource market pressures while imposing constraints on the unilateral actions of the firm,[5] we cannot confidently assert that the firm could establish efficient training.

We would expect that training would not satisfy efficiency conditions for a number of reasons. First, persons trained in specific skills have monopoly power over those skills. Through guts and bluff in labor negotiations, they may be able to extract a quasi-rent on those skills and receive a wage in excess of the market value of their general skills. They may also be able to force the firm to pay for part of their general training, which, for example, could explain why some firms reimburse tuition on night school courses. Second, entry ports to the firm,[6] the allocation of tasks within it and promotion possibilities are usually subject to rules established by mutual agreement, formal or informal, between employers and employees. These rules may require it to forego some training opportunities which would be efficient. Certainly, rules tend to be rigid in the short run, and this rigidity can impose an opportunity cost of profitable foregone training opportunities.

This is not intended to imply that the establishment of rules imposes only costs. Employees have interests in seniority rights, internal promotion and equitable treatment. Monopoly control of specific skills gives them leverage in establishing rules to defend those interests. The firm may also receive benefits because it has an interest in building employee loyalty and stabilizing its work force. With forces such as an employee's desire for equitable treatment, his monopoly over specific skills, and the firm's willingness to comply with some demands, we cannot expect that efficiency conditions for training, which depend on the uninhibited freedom of market forces, would be satisfied. For example, labor agreements may restrict the kinds of jobs that can be filled from the external labor market or may limit the transfer of employees across jobs. Obviously, such restrictions would affect the firm's decisions about how much training it will give to each employee for each task.

Considerations of efficiency however do impose constraints. If too many efficient training alternatives are foregone, then the firm's willingness to comply with existing rules may be changed into a determination to oppose those rules. Within the constraints imposed upon it, if a firm is concerned with profit maximization, we can conclude that an obvious relationship must exist between the willingness of a firm to hire and purchase training resources and the ability of the employee to increase his productivity. Finally while training decisions are constrained by labor agreements, we may reasonably assume that the hiring decision is controlled exclusively by the firm. Thus the decision as to whom it will hire into each of its entry port jobs is determined solely by the firm, which will hire a person so long as $NPDV_i > 0$.

Absenteeism

Absenteeism reduces $NPDV_i$ by reducing the number of time periods over which the firm receives the services of an employee. Assuming an employee is hired at time zero, terminates at T, and is never absent, Figure 1-1 represents net returns in each time period in the interval 1 to T, E_{it} being the cost of training inputs for any employee at any time t and W_{it} his wages at that time. Time τ is the period of zero returns. Prior to it, a worker's productivity is so low and his training costs so high that net returns are negative. Presumably a firm accepts negative returns over initial periods to get returns from a well trained worker in the future.

If a well trained employee is absent during period t'', $NPDV_i$ falls because the time periods of work within the interval t to T are reduced. The effect of early absenteeism, for example at t', is to postpone both returns and costs so that net benefits are less likely to occur. Assuming that a laborer must be on the job for t periods of training and work experience before the value of his output equals or exceeds expenditures on him in any time period, Figure 1-2 represents the effect

7

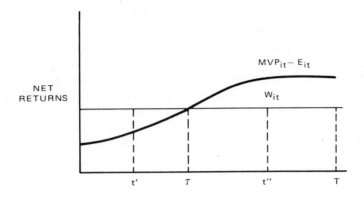

Figure 1-1. Net Returns at Each Point in Time.

of n periods of absenteeism, which does not reduce total undiscounted losses measured by the area between W_{it} and ($MVP_{it}-E_{it}$) prior to the period of zero returns. On the other hand n periods of absenteeism pushes the period of zero returns forward and reduces the periods during which the firm earns positive returns from ($T-\tau$) to $T-(\tau+n)$. Although absenteeism prior to the period of zero returns may postpone some losses as well as returns, it does not reduce undiscounted losses. But it does reduce undiscounted returns. Whether absenteeism occurs before or after the period of zero returns, discounted returns net of discounted losses, $NPDV_i$, are reduced.

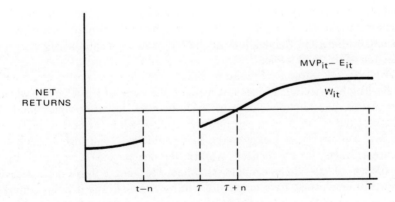

Figure 1-2. Absenteeism and Returns to a Firm.

Of course, absenteeism may cause internal adjustments. For example, if an employee is absent, a firm may minimize the reduction in output by juggling the distribution of tasks among its remaining labor force. This is covered within the definition of marginal value product, which is the reduction in output caused by an absence after the firm reallocated tasks in the most efficient manner. The firm may also respond to absenteeism by overmanning its plant. This imposes costs because training and screening expenditures are made simply to duplicate the services of absent employees. Nevertheless, a firm may find it profitable to overman given normal or expected rates of absenteeism. Since MVP_{it} is a decreasing function of the number working in any time period, it is basing its decision about the number hired on expected $NPDV_i$. The firm may hire additional persons only if expected $NPDV_i \geqslant 0$. With an uncertainty model where expected $NPDV_i$ is relevant to hiring decisions, an unexpectedly high incidence of absenteeism reduces the returns realized by the firm.

Turnover

Firms' preferences for stable, long-term employees readily capable of mastering their assigned tasks come from the desire to capitalize on recruitment, screening, and most important, training inputs invested in their employees. Termination of an employee establishes the limit of the return stream. Although $NPDV_i$ is a function of an employee's length of service with the firm, it may not be a monotonically increasing function of length of service. Over the initial periods of employment, $t' < \tau$ in Figure 1-1, marginal $NPDV_i$ with respect to length of service may be negative. This would occur because of very substantial training costs concentrated in the early periods. Even after training costs diminish and the worker's productivity increase and consequently marginal $NPDV_i$ becomes positive, many time periods may be required before the firm covers its investment and $NPDV_i$ become positive. So long as the firm sustains a loss over an initial hiring and training interval, $NPDV_i$ is not a monotonically increasing function of length of service.

While $NPDV_i$ measures the return stream from hiring a worker as a function of his length of service, it does not measure the costs of replacing him when he terminates. A distinction should be made between turnover, which limits the length of the return stream, and turnover cost, which is the cost of replacing a worker. Turnover cost measures the low productivity and high training costs incurred when an experienced worker terminates and is replaced by an inexperienced one. Some economists, when discussing a firm's preferences for long-term employees, have emphasized turnover costs. The relevant consideration as to whether a worker should be hired, however, is not the cost he imposes when and if he terminates but the opportunity cost of not hiring him. This opportunity cost is measured by the magnitude of $NPDV_i$. If a worker would remain aboard for a sufficient length of time so that $NPDV_i > 0$, then the worker should be hired.

Finally, length of service affects the willingness of a firm to invest training resources in its hires. As condition (1.1) indicates, the longer an employee's service, the greater the change in discounted returns given a marginal change in v_{it}^j. Whether marginal condition (1.1) is or is not strictly satisfied, an obvious relationship exists between the length of service and returns to training. This relationship leads to the conclusion: if the firm requires some minimal amount of training that it must purchase with its own funds, then that firm may not hire particularly transient persons at wages consistent with market value of the general skills when they apply to the firm. Such a wage rate may preclude the firm's recapturing its training costs over the transient employee's limited length of service. In other words, a negative net return over the initial periods of employment may be unavoidable, and a transient person may be too expensive to hire even at relatively low wage rates.

Heterogeneous Population of Job Applicants

The above discussion has assumed that the firm's applicant population was homogeneous in job performance when doing the same task or set of tasks. Thus any two applicants, given identical training, would perform identically. The firm need select only the optimal training program, which maximizes the discounted value of its return stream given constraints imposed by non-market forces, and continue to hire employees until $NPDV_m = 0$. More realistically, the firm is faced with selecting new employees from a heterogeneous population of applicants who differ in entry skills, length of service, absenteeism, and productivity.

For simplicity, assume that the firm is certain of the job performance of any employee whom it hires and trains and that applicants fall into two groups, x and y. The firm would select different training programs for each group, assigning members of the two groups to different jobs, and continue to hire employees until both $NPDV_{xm}$ and $NPDC_{ym}$ equal zero, where the subscripts refer to the marginal employees from the two groups. In specifying different jobs, we must be precise in what is meant by a job. It is a specific mix of tasks. If the firm faced no input constraints, in other words it could hire all it wished from both groups at a fixed wage, it would hire only from x or y to perform a job. At the same wage, persons from either x or y are more efficient in the performance of a specific mix of tasks, and applicants from one group would dominate those from the other. If however, the firm can divide its required tasks into different jobs, with wage differentials between the two groups, it may find it profitable to hire persons from both groups with each group assigned to a different job. For example, a firm may hire very experienced welders to perform sophisticated tasks, while at a lower wage rate it would be willing to hire persons with little or no welding experience to perform simpler tasks. If a firm allocates tasks in this manner, the production generated by an employee from one group is a function of the number hired from the other group. The equilibrium number of hires from both groups must be determined in a simultaneous solution with groups x and y considered distinctly different resources.

Production of output in period t is a function of the number of persons hired from both groups, the training resources invested over time in each, and fixed capital. If the production function is quasi-concave,[7] then we can determine isoquants with the usual properties for output in period t. This requires that one can trade off laborers from groups x and y at diminishing marginal rates of substitution. Furthermore, if $\overline{Q}_t$, a constant amount of output in period t, defines a convex set, then $\overline{Q}_t / (1+d)^t$ is also convex.

Of course, a decision at time zero to hire a particular number of persons from x and y results in specified levels of output ($Q_O, \ldots, Q_T$). Assume that while the firm pays for its labor inputs and realizes output over several periods, it commits itself at time zero. Thus its decision at zero determines total output over time. One can isolate combinations of inputs at time zero for which

$$(1.2) \qquad \overline{Q} = \sum_{t=1}^{T} \frac{Q_t}{(1+d)^t}$$

where $\overline{Q}$ is a constant. This requires merely summing across convex sets, the result being a convex set. Isoquants described by (1.2) must be non-intersecting so long as the addition of one laborer adds to or at least does not subtract from total output for every time period during which he remains aboard. Since this is an assumed characteristic of the production function, isoquants are convex and non-intersecting.

A decision at time zero also commits the firm to costs over time. Since one can determine costs over time as the sum of initial period recruitment and screening costs and the stream of discounted wage and training costs, one could also describe isocost lines. The analysis of labor allocation decisions by firms with the human capital model is not very different from analyses with traditional wage theory. Analyses under both are consistent with concepts such as constrained maximization, convex sets, and marginal rates of substitution, and the following discussion of the possible effects of manpower programs for the disadvantaged will be phrased in terms of these traditional wage theory concepts. The only difference between traditional wage theory and human capital theory for discussions of profit maximizing resource allocations is that human capital theory is more general, emphasizing the time dimension and including cost parameters not considered in traditional wage theory.

Implications of the Human Capital
Model for Manpower Programs

Given wage levels, training resource prices, and output prices, the firm can determine a profit-maximizing combination of new employees from groups x and y, hiring from both at different wages even if persons from y offered relatively poor job performance. Furthermore, an increasing demand for labor and a fixed supply of reliable applicants could lead to the hiring of more less reliable persons to perform more tasks. The resulting availability of entry port jobs for less reliable or less skilled persons may subsequently make available even more sophisticated and better paying jobs because training resources are being invested in them. This could both generate promotion possibilities within the firm and make such persons more attractive in the labor market external to the firm that does the training. Thus wage differentials between the two groups could narrow over time. Most important, such a tendency would become more common as labor markets tightened. This statement is consistent with the views of Piore,[8] and Doeringer and Piore.[9] They do not support the contention that unemployment is structural. Firms do provide the training to integrate less qualified employees into the job structure of their plants. Of course, Doeringer and Piore note that such training would raise unit costs. With a queue theory of the labor market, the hiring and training of less reliable employees would be most common in a tight labor market when more reliable laborers become scarce. Piore maintains that if bottlenecks develop, management will seek out relatively less scarce kinds of labor.

While such a process should increase the wage income of less reliable or less skilled employees, it is by no means clear that the wage gains of such persons would increase compared to the wage gains of the relatively more scarce, reliable or otherwise, productive employees. Yet the gap in income between urban poor, especially blacks, and other kinds of labor does narrow as the economy approaches full employment.[10] This suggests that the gap in productivity narrows, which requires increased training opportunities for urban poor as the labor market tightens. Thus, macroeconomic data on the change in relative incomes as the economy approaches full employment is consistent with microeconomic studies on the adjustments made by firms as labor become scarce.

If manpower programs are intended to increase the training and employment opportunities of urban poor, such programs must operate in an economy where training opportunities already exist. This is not intended to imply that market-induced training opportunities are adequate to generate a satisfactory intra-temporal income distribution. It does imply that manpower program administrators should be sensitive to existing training opportunities. Administrators should be aware that their programs are not simply creating opportunities where none previously existed. Manpower programs can be an effective technique for altering both the magnitude and distribution of income only if they either increase the number of persons receiving training or create access to higher wage jobs by increasing the amount of training given to any one person. Most important, if manpower administrators are to use their limited public funds to most effectively achieve their purposes, they must avoid the duplication of training opportunities that would have been initiated by firms in the absence of manpower programs.

The Distribution of the Output of Manpower Programs

Having outlined the effect of variables relevant to a firm's hiring, training, and promotion decision, we now procede to a theoretical analysis of the effect of manpower program subsidies on these decisions. To facilitate the analysis some unrealistic simplifying assumptions will be made. These assumptions will subsequently be changed to more accurately depict the legal restrictions and institutional structures of manpower programs.

Under Wage Subsidies

Assume that a government agency is considering upgrading the employment of persons from group y. It chooses to do so by offering subsidies for their employment in an entry port job. For the moment, assume that this is by a simple payment per hire. This payment is made to a contracting firm which receives a subsidy of s dollars per hire from group y up to a limit of sY^* dollars, where Y^* represents the limit of the number of persons whom the government will cover. Assume also that the subsidy does not directly affect the firm's allocation of screening and training resources—that it is a wage subsidy.[11] Although these assumptions will be altered to consider the impact of programs, both institutional and on-the-job, which do affect the allocation of screening and training resources, the simplifying assumptions do not alter essential conclusions.

While the firm is subsidized up to Y^* hires for one entry port job, it may have chosen to hire at least some persons from group y for that job without the inducement of subsidies. This could occur because with its existing wage structure either persons from Y are the more profitable alternative or persons from x are not available in sufficient numbers. Defining $\hat{Y}$ to be number of persons who would have been hired for a particular entry port job without subsidies, one can show that manpower programs may benefit firms that are operating under any of the three following conditions:

(1.3) $\hat{Y} = 0$

(1.4) $Y^* > \hat{Y} > 0$, and

(1.5) $\hat{Y} \geqslant Y^*$.

The conclusions about the distributional impacts of manpower programs are dependent upon which of the three possible conditions reflects the hiring decisions that the firm would have made in the absence of the subsidy program. The analysis includes how the firm would have operated under conditions (1.3), (1.4), and finally under (1.5).

Assuming $\hat{Y} = 0$. A government agency has three alternatives when establishing both a subsidy per employee and the maximum number to be subsidized. Both may be set arbitrarily by the agency, negotiated with the firm, or based on detailed investigation of the costs imposed on a firm when it hires from group y. Such cost estimates require data on training inputs, rates of absenteeism and turnover, and productivity of persons from group y at a job or jobs within the firm being considered for subsidies. Given this information, a manpower program administrator could simultaneously set the limit, Y^*, and the subsidy per hire that would induce the firm to hire up to that limit while imposing a minimum cost of the program. Manpower program administrators do not have the information required to establish simultaneously limits and payments per hire so that costs are at a minimum and the limit is reached. Generally, the conditions of the manpower contract are established through negotiations with the firm; but however they are established, the firm would adjust at the margin so that

(1.6) $$MRTS_{x/y} \leqslant \frac{p_x}{p_y - s}$$

where

(a) $MRTS_{x/y}$ is the marginal rate of technical substitution; and
(b) p_y for example, is the discounted cost stream associated with the hiring of any person from group y.

Either of two outcomes is consistent with the establishment of an equality between $MRTS_{x/y}$ and the subsidized price ratio. The equality could result at some number of hires Y', where $Y' < Y^*$; or it could occur at $Y' = Y^*$. In the former, the subsidy is so small that the constraint on the number of persons who could receive subsidies is not binding. In the latter, the subsidy is just sufficient to induce the firm to hire up to the limit, Y^*.

In both outcomes the firm would earn net returns greater than those that would have been earned in the absence of the subsidy. The necessary condition for the firm to get returns from the program is simply that over some subset of intramarginal employees from group y, $MRTS_{x/y} < P_x/P_y - s$. With an increasing $MRTS_{x/y}$, a sufficient condition is that the subsidy payment, s, is the same for each employee. Since $MRTS_{x/y}$ increases as the number of persons hired from group y increases, $MRTS_{x/y}$ must be less than $p_x/p_y - s$ over the set of intramarginal hires $(1, \ldots, y, \ldots, Y'-1)$. In other words, the total subsidy payment to the firm for the set of intramarginal employees exceeds that amount that is required to compensate the firm for the costs it accepts when it substitutes hires from group y for hires from group x.

Nevertheless, if $Y' < Y^*$ individuals are hired, one can be confident that the subsidy paid for the employment of Y' will not exceed that amount required to insure employment up to Y', because if s falls, then the number hired from group y also falls. Therefore, the cost in public funds required to achieve the employment and training of Y' is at a minimum given the constraint that all persons are subsidized by the same amount. Furthermore, if stockholders receive benefits only because intramarginal employees are subsidized at the marginal rate, the amount of income accruing to stockholders may be insignificant relative to the benefits for persons who received employment under the program. However, the firm may also receive an excess subsidy at the margin, because the agencies administering the programs may be unaware of the true costs of hiring persons eligible for subsidies.

In general, manpower programs benefit shareholders. These benefits may occur simply because intramarginal employees are subsidized at the marginal rate, but subsidies may also be excessive at the margin. This conclusion is not sufficient to argue that the equity impacts of manpower programs are so perverse the programs are socially undesirable. If a program transferred income to shareholders only because intramarginal employees are subsidized at the marginal rate, the perverse equity effect is likely to be extremely small compared to income gains for the disadvantaged. Even if the subsidized price ratio differed substantially from the $MRTS_{x/y}$ at the limit Y^*, the program may be socially desirable; although given an ethical preference for an equitable distribution of consumption, it may be improved by reducing the subsidy payments. Whether a manpower program is or is not socially desirable or can or cannot be improved is both an empirical and ethical question. The theoretical discussion presented in this section is intended merely to indicate that even if a firm would not have hired from group y for a particular job without subsidies, that firm would still receive some increment to earnings as a result of the subsidy.

Assuming $Y^* > \hat{Y} > 0$. The above discussion has assumed that in the absence of subsidies, no workers from group y would have been hired into jobs for which the firm received subsidies. Such need not be true. If labor market conditions create a situation in which some persons from group y should have been hired without subsidies, the firm could be receiving subsidies for persons it would have hired anyway. This section will analyze the impact of a manpower program under assumption (1.4), that is, the firm would have hired some number from group y less than Y^*.

Most important, the benefits to group y that are a direct result of subsidies cannot be measured by consumption gains accruing to all subsidized persons. The subsidy payments generate wage benefits to $(Y' - \hat{Y})$ persons, where Y' refers to the number of persons actually hired to perform a given job, and where $\hat{Y}$ refers to the number of persons who would have been hired to perform that job if the manpower program had not been instituted. The following discussion will demonstrate that

(1.8) $\qquad Y' \leqslant Y^*.$

Thus at best the manpower program generates employment for only $(Y^* - \hat{Y})$ persons, because the firm would not hire beyond the limit of the subsidy.

The validity of statement (1.8) can easily be demonstrated. Consider the problem of profit maximization subject to a production function constraint.

(1.9) $\quad$ Max $\pi = pq - p_x x - p_y y_n - p_y y_s - p_k \bar{k}.$

(1.10) $\qquad$ s.t. $Q = f(x, y_n + y_s, \bar{k}).$

We know that prior to the introduction of the subsidy,

(1.11) $\qquad y_n = \hat{y}$, and

(1.12) $\qquad y_s = 0.$

We can introduce a subsidy and reformulate the problem as

(1.13) $\quad$ Max $\pi = pq - p_x x - p_y y_n - (p_s - s)y_s - p_k \bar{k}.$

(1.14) $\qquad$ s.t. $y_s \leqslant Y^*$

and subject to (1.10).

Given any subsidy payment, s, and any quota, Y^*, the firm could adjust at the margin to either of the following two outcomes: (a) $(p_y - s)/p_x = f_y/f_x$ and $p_y/p_x > f_y/f_x$; or (b) $(p_y - s)/p_x < f_y/f_x$ and $p_y/p_x > f_y/f_x$. In (a) the limit of the subsidy may or may not be exhausted, but the firm would not be willing to hire any nonsubsidized persons because the ratio of non-subsidized price to the price of x is greater than the $MRTS_{x/y}$. Case (b) would occur only if (1.14) were a binding constraint. Then the firm would be willing to hire more persons from y

given the subsidy per hire, but once again, it would not be willing to hire any additional person from y without a subsidy. Thus, in either (a) or (b), y_n would fall to zero. The result of the subsidy program would be a one to one substitution of y_s for y_n.

The firm adjusts to either conditions (a) or (b). No other alternative is consistent with the assumption that $Y^* > \hat{Y}$. The only conceivable alternative to (a) and (b) is adjustment by the firm so that at the margin $p_y/p_x = f_y/f_x$. This however implies that

(1.15) $f_y = p_y/p$, and

(1.16) $f_x = p_x/p$

But with capital constant and assuming all factors exhibit diminishing marginal returns, (1.15) and (1.16) can be simultaneously valid only at the pre-subsidy equilibrium, and thus are inconsistent with the assumption that $Y^* > \hat{Y}$. Since the firm would adjust only to condition (a) or (b), causing a one to one substitution of y_s for y_n, the subsidy program increases employment no more than ($Y^* - \hat{Y}$). Taxpayers pay sY^*, but benefits accrue to only ($Y^* - \hat{Y}$) employees.

The firm receiving a subsidy on total hires up to Y^* is realizing the benefit of a lump sum transfer. The firm can transfer $\hat{Y}$ persons into the subsidy program, hire only $\hat{Y}$, leaving its output and pricing decisions unaffected, and consequently not alter its presubsidy profit maximizing position. It merely receives a payment of $s\hat{Y}$. Quite obviously it alters its pre-subsidy equilibrium by hiring an additional ($Y^* - \hat{Y}$) persons in response to the additional subsidy payment it can receive on the ($Y^* - \hat{Y}$) persons. The subsidy payment on these persons also represents a source of benefits to shareholders so long as the firm is paid the same amount, s, for each hire, and the production function exhibits diminishing marginal rates of substitution. At best, the intramarginal incremental hires are being subsidized at the marginal rate.

On the other hand, ($Y^* - \hat{Y}$) jobs for the disadvantaged are created. The benefits from these jobs may more than offset the perverse effect of the transfer from taxpayers to shareholders. Whether the program is or is not socially desirable is an empirical question. But as the difference between Y^* and $\hat{Y}$ becomes smaller, the benefits for the disadvantaged diminish while the perverse equity effect grows.

Assuming $Y^* \geqslant \hat{Y}$. Previously, we have assumed that a firm would hire either no workers or only a limited number of workers from group y. No legal restrictions would deny manpower subsidies to firms who hire a substantial number of their labor force from group y. In the absence of legal restrictions, manpower program administrators when assessing contracts generally do not ask this question:

would subsidized persons have been hired to perform a given job without subsidies? No reason exists to assume that manpower contracts would not be let to firms represented under condition (1.5), that is, the number of persons who would have been hired without subsidies exceeds Y^*.

If condition (1.5) is valid, the subsidy would be a lump sum transfer. No hires from group y in excess of those the firm would have made anyway are necessary to receive the entire subsidy payment, sY^*. In other words the firm would not be required to deviate from its pre-subsidy output and employment level, and the entire subsidy could be used to defray labor costs that the firm would have profitably accepted without subsidies. The subsidy program yields no benefits to persons from group y because all of them would have been hired without subsidies. The impact of the program is to generate income and consumption benefits for shareholders. Most important, if one can observe $Y' > Y^*$, this implies that at the margin conditions (1.15) and (1.16) hold. But those two conditions hold only at the pre-subsidy equilibrium, and one can therefore conclude that the manpower program had no impact on the employment of y, that is, $\hat{Y} = Y' > Y^*$.

The Firms that Would Seek Manpower Subsidies. Firms which would have hired from group y in the absence of subsidies would have an incentive to seek such subsidies. If a firm would not hire men from group y in the absence of subsidies, it must be offered some minimum subsidy before it will willingly add one such new employee. The minimum subsidy it requires may be substantial. On the other hand, a firm that could have hired persons from group y without subsidies finds itself in a highly favorable position. No matter how small the subsidy per employee, such a firm could reduce its costs from those it would have hired anyway. To the extent that firms engage in such a profitable activity, one must reduce the total wage benefits credited to manpower programs by that number of employees that did not require a subsidy to be hired or promoted.

The hypotheses that firms receive at least some returns from manpower programs and that firms hiring the disadvantaged without subsidies have an incentive to use manpower programs have been derived from a model that assumes a certain world. These hypotheses would not be significantly changed if an uncertainty model would have been developed. Admittedly, in an uncertain world we would expect to observe some firms losing money from their association with a manpower program. This may be especially true of firms without prior experience with the disadvantaged and consequently without first hand knowledge of their work habits and productivity. But if firms are risk averters, they would only cooperate in a manpower program if their expected returns were positive. Furthermore, risk aversion only increases the likelihood that firms associated with manpower programs will be those with previous experience in hiring the disadvantaged. Besides, for a firm that would have hired the disadvantaged without subsidies, hiring them under a subsidy program reduces the probability of a loss.

Theoretical arguments indicate that, in general, firms receive some share of the benefits that are generated by manpower programs. The firm's share may be minimal; but if it would have hired many persons from group y without subsidies, its share of the benefits may be substantial, with enrollees receiving little or no incremental earnings as a result of the program. Substantial benefits are naturally an incentive to firms to seek a manpower contract.

Under Training Subsidies[1][2]

In the previous section we discussed the impact of a wage subsidy, assuming that the firm received a simple payment per hire that it chose to credit against wage costs. In this section we will discuss the slightly more complicated problem of a subsidy tied to the purchase of training resources. We no longer need assume that the firm receives a direct payment. Although a direct payment may occur through an on-the-job program, the resources may be purchased through institutional pre-employment programs. The essential consideration is that public funds are tied to the purchase of training resources.

It will be argued that, in general, the conclusions developed in the previous section about the impact of untied subsidies are relevant to tied training subsidies. Training subsidies do, however, exhibit unique aspects that will be discussed in some detail. Most important among these, a tied training subsidy as opposed to an untied subsidy may increase program costs without substantially increasing benefits. Second, although both wage and training subsidies increase the employment from group y, dollar for dollar, a training subsidy cannot result in more employment from y as opposed to an untied subsidy program.

The Excess Program Costs Imposed by Tied Subsidies. Given that the firm could allocate subsidy payments to either wage or training costs in any time period, it would choose to credit the subsidy against only the price of a training resource if this resulted in incremental returns in excess of a simple deduction from wages. If the price of training resources j is reduced by s_j, then the net price to the firm is (p_j-s_j). Subject to constraints imposed by non-market forces discussed in a previous section, the amount of resources purchased to train the ith individual are determined by the net price. However, the purchase of an increment of a training resource in period t, caused by the reduction in its price, would be made only if the resulting increment to discounted marginal value product were at least equal to $s_j/(1+d)^t$. If not, s_j would be deducted from wages and additional purchases of training resources would not be made. Of course if the pre-subsidy training program of a firm were efficient, then dollar for dollar the firm would always prefer a simple payment per hire, that is, a wage subsidy. However, the argument that dollar for dollar the firm would prefer an untied subsidy is not dependent on the efficiency of pre-subsidy training. It is dependent only on the assertion that by tying the subsidy, we restrict the opportunities of the firm. Thus, tying the subsidy can force the firm to engage in an inferior activity, that is formal on-the-job or institutional training, when it would prefer to use the funds in some other activity.

Manpower programs do not offer simple payments per hire that the firm can credit either against the price of training resources at the margin or against wages. A manpower program subsidizes only certain specified training resources for a specified number of persons. If the objective of the manpower program is to use public funds to provide either entry port or upgraded jobs for the disadvantaged, then forcing the purchase of training resources with those funds can only increase the public funds that must be expended. When funds must be used for training, whether on-the-job or institutional, the cost to gain the compliance of any firm cannot be less than and may be more than the expenditures that would be required with direct untied payments per hire. Under such circumstances, training subsidies may only increase program costs without increasing program benefits.

Possible Benefits from Tying Subsidies to Training. The excess costs from subsidies tied to training can be justified only if any increased training results in increased output with a social value exceeding the excess social costs caused by tying subsidies. Notice, however, that judging whether the tying of subsidies is socially desirable or undesirable does not hinge solely upon the question of economic efficiency, that is, the magnitude of program output, but it is also a function of who receives the consumption benefits generated by that output. If we value equity, then the social value of any output caused by tied subsidies would be larger if the benefits accrue primarily to the trainees rather than to the shareholders. In fact it may be essential that benefits accrue to trainees, because if the firm is reasonably efficient, the increment to the returns of firm and shareholders from training resource purchases forced by tied subsidies may not offset the excess program costs of tying the subsidy program.

However, increments to the purchase of training resources induced by tied subsidies need not increase the wage benefits of trainees. If, for example, the labor market were perferctly competitive, then wage gains require that the subsidized formal training increase the purchase of resources for general training. The inducement to increase such purchases may be minimal. Even if the firm would realize some returns from the general skills of intramarginal employees, all the benefits of specific skills would accrue to it rather than to employees in a competitive resource market. Thus, even in a perfectly competitive world, one could not simply assume that incremental purchases of resources for training cause increments to wages.

Of course, labor resource markets are not perfectly competitive, because wages are determined and fixed through negotiation. Negotiated agreements usually have common characteristics. The wage is determined by the job within the job structure of the plant. Two persons performing the same job receive the same wages regardless of differences in abilities. Wage increases by promotion are generally limited by seniority and by the structure of jobs within a plant. Under these circumstances, if some increase in training induced by tying subsidies in either institutional or on-the-job programs does not affect a person's entry port job, then one would not expect that incremental purchases of training resources, even if used to create general skills, would result in incremental earnings by subsidized hires.

There are two exceptions where incremental purchases could create increments to earnings without affecting a trainee's entry port job. First, for piece rates, if tying subsidies increases productivity, then the earnings of both the trainees and the firm would increase. Second, a firm may pay wages as a function of the skill level that an employee can apply to any job, regardless of the job classification. Once again, increments to training may cause increments to earnings. But this requires that incremental training from tied subsidies raises the skill level enough to justify higher wages even if it does not affect the entry port job.

A tied subsidy program may not increase wages compared to a simple direct payment per hire. If tying the subsidies does not affect a person's entry port job or access to promotion and if wages are determined by a person's job classification, then tying the subsidies would increase a trainee's earnings only if a firm raised its wage structure in response to the high productivity of the trainees. But a firm would most probably not shift up its entire wage structure to accommodate some small percentage of its work force that received subsidized training. The point is that if a firm increases the wages offered to subsidized persons for a given job, it must increase the wages offered to every person performing that job. Costs could be prohibitive. Likewise, training may not increase access to promotions. One would not expect management to rearrange its internal job structure and access to promotions to the detriment of its existing labor force simply to accommodate a few subsidized trainees.

Increased training may simply provide returns to the subsidized firm as the benefits of the increased training, either general or specific, accrue to it. Of course, the firm may have to accept more turnover if it attempts to use employees with more marketable skills without offering them higher wages. So long as labor is not perfectly mobile, the firm may be willing to accept some increase in turnover if it can benefit from the greater productivity of those who remain. Labor is not completely immobile and some trainees may benefit from improved marketable skills. But the wage benefits of increased marketable skills caused by tied subsidies accrue to only a subgroup of subsidized trainees. In subsidized on-the-job training, it may accrue only to those among the subsidized who terminate their employment with the subsidized firm and use their new skills in subsequent employment. In institutional training, benefits from tied subsidies would accrue to trainees only when the incremental training they received because of the tied program was essential to acquire their subsequent employment. Thus the benefits of increased training resource purchases may accrue only to persons whose training is in general skills, and even then the benefits may accrue to only a small number of the persons trained. On the other hand, it is conceivable that a very substantial proportion of the benefits, even from increased general training, may accrue to the firm.

Tied formal training subsidies need not result in wage gains greater than those that could be made through a simple payment for hiring a worker. The remainder of this section will demonstrate that conclusions about the possible distribution of manpower program benefits derived under the assumption of a wage subsidy are applicable to a training subsidy.

The Distribution of Outputs from Training Subsidies. We will first consider $\hat{Y} \geqslant Y^*$, where $\hat{Y}$ is the number of persons from group y who would be hired without subsidies to perform a given job and Y^* is the number of persons who can be subsidized. In this circumstance, a training subsidy has an impact similar to a wage subsidy at the margin; that is, the training subsidy would have no impact at the margin. With $\hat{Y} \geqslant Y^*$, a manpower program that subsidizes certain specified training resources for a limited number of persons need not generate improved employment opportunities for the trainees; and the manpower program may not generate any benefits for such persons because it does not affect a firm's marginal decisions.

The training subsidy is different in one respect from a simple payment per hire. Given a simple payment per hire, if $\hat{Y} \geqslant Y^*$, the firm has no inducement to alter its pre-subsidy training decisions over all persons from group y. On the other hand, given a tied training subsidy, even if $\hat{Y} \geqslant Y^*$, where $\hat{Y}$ is the marginal hire, the subsidized training, over the range of intramarginal hires up to Y^*, may be somewhat different from the training program that would be established without subsidies. This difference could impose an opportunity cost on the firm. The cost would be reflected in the firm's preferences, where a dollar of a training subsidy is worth less to it than a simple dollar payment. Thus tying subsidies to training may not increase benefits to trainees. It may only reduce the total benefits of the program by reducing those benefits that shareholders receive from a dollar of public funds allocated to a manpower program.

Where $0 \leqslant \hat{Y} < Y^*$, the subsidies may be sufficient to affect a firm's marginal decisions. If Y^* persons are hired, then ($Y^* - \hat{Y}$) trainees do receive benefits from the program. Of course no more than Y^* persons would be hired for the reasons presented above in the discussion of conditions (1.15) and (1.16). However, once again a training subsidy has an impact somewhat different from a payment per hire. The manpower program, whether on the job or institutional, affects the hiring decisions of firms by reducing the price to the firm of training resources if it hires certain persons. If the program is to affect the firm's hiring decisions, then at the margin the price of some subsidized training resource, j, is $(p_j - s_j)$, where the jth resource is used to train an individual from group y. The production function is defined across labor, x, y, and training resources. Reducing the price of training resource j at the margin introduces a substitution effect. This substitution effect would induce the firm to substitute training resource j for some unsubsidized training resource k. More important, the substitution effect also exists between training resources and labor inputs. A firm would be induced to substitute training resources, which make a given number of laborers more productive, for more labor. Training subsidies can induce a firm to hire more persons from group y than they would hire without subsidies. However, since training subsidies generate a substitution effect, a given dollar expenditure of public funds could generate less employment for group y than a simple payment per hire.

To review briefly, tying subsidies to training resource purchases may be desirable if the social value is sufficient to offset the incremental social costs that result solely from the tying of the subsidy. Whether or not tied subsidies are socially preferable to simple payments per hire is an empirical question; however, one can make general statements about the possible results from the tying of subsidies. The tying of subsidies to training need not increase benefits to trainees over a simple payment to a firm per hire. Tying subsidies to training resource purchases may introduce a substitution effect of training for labor. Consequently, dollar for dollar, a payment per hire may generate more employment for group y than would be realized with subsidies that reduce the price of training resources.[13]

Firms that Would Seek Training Subsidies. In the section on wage subsidies, we argued that firms that did not require subsidies to hire from group y might be tempted to seek subsidies. This conclusion remains valid for training subsidies because a firm that would have hired and trained group y for a given job without subsidies may be able to transfer to taxpayers a substantial proportion of those training costs that it could have profitably absorbed. The subsidies that it receives directly for on-the-job training or indirectly when it hires the graduates of an institutional manpower program need only be large enough to generate some increment in the returns of the firm. If, on the other hand, another firm would not have hired from group y, we can reasonably presume that such persons would generate a negative return (possibly substantially negative) to a firm choosing not to pay the training and wage costs required to integrate such persons into their job structure. To induce such a firm to hire from group y, the subsidies may have to be substantial, because the subsidy program must generate more than simply some marginal increment in returns. The subsidy program would have to cover at least the negative returns such persons would generate. Thus while firms that would not have hired from group y to perform a given job might require a substantial subsidy, a firm that would have hired and trained group y without subsidies for a given job could be expected to find relatively small subsidies attractive.

Formal training programs have been subsidized in part because training costs are easily identifiable, but this is in itself no virtue. Formal training programs neither eliminate the possibility of substantial consumption transfers between taxpayers and shareholders, nor do they assure wage gains to employees greater than those which could be acquired through a wage subsidy. A training subsidy may, however, impose an excess cost on taxpayers.

Summary and Conclusions

Turnover, absenteeism, and productivity affect the returns of a firm. In the human capital model, productivity is a function of the training resources that a firm invests in its employees. Thus the firm would have a relative preference for productive employees capable of mastering their tasks quickly and at minimum training cost. The problem of turnover is important because training and screening costs during the initial periods of employment must be compensated by extended employment. Absenteeism has an effect similar to turnover in that it limits the number of time periods over which the firm can earn returns from any employee.

Although logically a firm prefers stable, reliable employees, populations of job applicants are neither homogeneous across firms nor within a firm. Firms must therefore invest funds to screen applicants and consider the most profitable way to divide the required tasks among them, where definable groups could be expected to perform very differently when assigned to any given job. In such a situation and with wage differentials, the firm may hire at least some persons who could be expected to offer poor job performances because competitive bidding for reliable employees has made it profitable to do so. Even if wages are fixed in the short run, such that competitive wage bidding could be considered only a rather sluggish long-run adjustment, any firm may find it impossible to recruit at a given wage all of the more reliable, stable employees that it would wish. Given this situation, once again, the firm might find it profitable to hire and train at least some less reliable employees. This is not intended to imply that less reliable or less productive employees would be assigned to the same task or set of tasks as more reliable ones. In general, the firm profits from assigning such persons to tasks requiring relatively small training inputs. But as aggregate demand increases and the labor market tightens, a firm may be forced to hire more persons who are relatively less scarce in the labor market, such as ghetto residents. Once hired, such persons begin to accumulate the seniority rights and specific skills that could induce the firm both to invest additional training resources in them and to promote them rather than seek other employees from the external labor market. This is not intended to suggest that training opportunities for the urban poor are adequate from a normative standpoint, but simply that such opportunities exist.

Manpower programs are intended to increase the number of employment and training opportunities available to definable subgroups of the population. They do this by subsidizing, either directly or indirectly, firms prepared to hire such persons. Programs affect both efficiency and equity. A subsidy program that alters the hiring and training decisions of the firm may be efficient, but the more efficient the firm prior to subsidies, the less likely that the subsidy program would generate efficiency benefits to offset the social costs of the program.[14] However, given market and non-market distortions which affect the firm's internal allocation of jobs, promotions, and training resources, we cannot assert that any firm is allocating training resources efficiently.

In general, a perverse transfer of at least some income and consumption benefits is unavoidable in manpower programs. If they are also distributing benefits to the poor, the undesirable aspects of the programs (the redistribution in favor of shareholders and, if it exists, the efficiency loss) may be more than offset by equity benefits. Of course, a judgment as to whether any manpower program has been socially desirable may be difficult. Given that a program may be more or less efficient and may combine perverse and desirable redistribution impacts, such a judgment would require both detailed information and explicit ethical statements. But even after the information is processed and the ethical statements are made, the one who judges may still feel uneasy about his decision because he may have been forced to trade-off desirable and undesirable impacts of the program.

Most important, before any judgment can be made, information must be provided about the equity impacts of the programs. Employment cost studies must be made on firms that have used labor trained under manpower programs. These studies must be designed to measure the costs incurred by the firm and any differences between costs and subsidy levels. While such studies would be helpful in assessing the efficiency impacts of manpower programs, they are essential to an investigation of the equity impacts. In stating that cost studies must be performed, we must indicate precisely what cost or costs are relevant. We are not interested merely in the cost of training resources but with relating training, absenteeism, turnover, and low productivity costs to the returns of the firm. The cost that ultimately concerns us is the opportunity cost in reduced returns when and if the firm substitutes employees eligible for subsidies for those that the firm would have hired without subsidies. This cost must be compared to the benefits accruing to the firm from the subsidy program, and the comparison allows judgment of the program's impact on the returns of a surveyed firm. Most important, we must also assess the firm's hiring and promotion criteria to determine whether persons hired under the subsidy program would have been acceptable for employment in those same jobs that they presumably acquired because of the subsidies.

25

Notes

1. See Gary S. Becker, HUMAN CAPITAL: A THEORETICAL AND EMPIRICAL ANALYSIS WITH SPECIAL REFERENCE TO EDUCATION (New York: Columbia University Press, 1964); and Walter Oi, "Labor as a Quasi-fixed Factor," THE JOURNAL OF POLITICAL ECONOMY 70 (Dec., 1962): 538-555.

2. Peter B. Doeringer and Michael J. Piore, INTERNAL LABOR MARKETS AND MANPOWER ANALYSIS (Lexington, Mass.: Heath Lexington Books, 1971).

3. For an extensive discussion of general and specific training see Becker, HUMAN CAPITAL.

4. If training were general, MVP_{it} would represent a return to the employee as opposed to the firm. But since p_j would represent a cost to the employee, the first order conditions would be unchanged. The only additional consideration would be that the employee's rate of time preference would differ from the firm's rate of return on reinvested capital. Thus, d_i, the ith individual's rate of time preference may differ from d, the firm's rate of return on reinvested funds.

5. This book will not go into the details of the structure of the internal labor market. The interested reader may refer to Doeringer and Piore, INTERNAL LABOR MARKETS; Richard A. Lester, HIRING PRACTICES AND LABOR COMPETITION (Princeton, N.J.: Princeton University Press, 1954); and Lloyd Reynolds, THE STRUCTURE OF LABOR MARKETS (New York: Harper & Brothers, 1951).

6. Not all jobs in a plant are open to persons from the outside because of either employer preferences or institutional rules. Many are filled by promotions from within. Those jobs that are available to people on the outside are called entry ports. See Clark Kerr, "The Balkanization of Labor Markets," LABOR MOBILITY AND ECONOMIC OPPORTUNITY, ed. by E. Wright Bakke (Cambridge, Mass.: MIT Press, 1954), 92-110.

7. See Kenneth Arrow and Alain Enthoven, "Quasi-Concave Programming," ECONOMETRICA 29 (Oct., 1961); 785-797.

8. Michael J. Piore, "Impact of Labor Markets on the Design and Selection of Productive Technique within the Manufacturing Plant," QUARTERLY JOURNAL OF ECONOMICS 62 (Nov., 1968); 602-620.

9. Peter Doeringer and Michael J. Piore, "Labor Market Adjustment and Internal Training," PROCEEDINGS OF THE EIGHTEENTH ANNUAL MEETING, Industrial Relation Research Association, (1965), 250-263.

10. See for example W.H.L. Anderson, "Trickling Down: The Relationship between Economic Growth and the Extent of Poverty Among American Families," QUARTERLY JOURNAL OF ECONOMICS, (Nov., 1964), 511-524; and Lester C. Thurow, "The Changing Structure of Unemployment: An Economic Study," REVIEW OF ECONOMICS AND STATISTICS 47 (May, 1965; 137-149.

11. Given the assumption of a wage subsidy, it is not necessary to discuss the impact of that subsidy on opening promotion possibilities for the subsidized wage earners. It is assumed that an entry port job is specifically tied to a set of promotion possibilities. If access to the entry port job is created through the subsidy program, then access to subsequent promotions is also made available through the wage subsidy. However, when training subsidies are discussed, access to promotion will be explicitly considered. Tying subsidies may increase the training received relative to a wage subsidy and may improve job performance. If this does occur, then tied training subsidies may create access to promotions that would not be forthcoming under a wage subsidy.

12. The subsequent discussion of training programs that only screen applicants and the conclusions are in no way affected by substituting the word "screening" for "training."

13. Of course, subsidizing particular training resources may increase the demand for them. If this increases the market price of such resources or draws unemployed training resources into production, then the tied subsidy program does generate benefits for the owners of such resources. This effect may or may not exist, and if it does, it may or may not be sufficient to alter our judgment as to whether such programs are socially desirable. Of course, training programs were not established to increase the consumption of the owners of training resources.

14. The careful reader would have noticed that the question of externalities has not been considered. For example, increasing the income of the urban poor may reduce crime or drug addiction. It may benefit the children of the urban poor. These externalities, if they exist, are logically a function of the amount of income generated for such persons under the manpower programs. One can reasonably conclude that if a manpower program generates little or no consumption benefits for the poor, then the external benefits that it generates would be minimal.

2

Design of Manpower Program Studies

Having developed the basic theory for understanding manpower programs, we may find it instructive to look briefly at some cost-benefit studies, all of which conclude that manpower programs are socially desirable. Yet the material does suggest that, in accord with the arguments presented in the previous chapter, benefits accruing to trainees may have been minimal and benefits accruing to shareholders may have been significant. Arguments for this position will be offered for three of the best known studies, those of Borus,[1] Somers,[2] and Somers and Stromsdorfer.[3] Finally, a recent study by Hardin and Borus[4] will be discussed in detail because it is one of the best available, exceptionally complete with unusual amounts of raw data, which allows a thorough analysis of their results.

Although the studies are dissimilar in many assumptions they make about the duration and magnitude of program costs and benefits, they are similar to the extent that none investigate the firms that hire trainees.[5] Because they do not, they may give overestimates of efficiency impacts and cannot provide information about equity impacts. To eliminate potential overestimates and to get information about the distribution of benefits, a study should be constructed to be consistent with the theoretical arguments presented in the previous chapter. This can be accomplished using data that firms often collect as a normal business activity. We will indicate how such data will be used in the study of two firms to avoid shortcomings in analyses of manpower programs.

The General Approach of Manpower Cost-Benefit Studies

Existing cost-benefit studies compare the gain in earnings of trainees against the dollar value of resources purchased with public funds. Estimates of the gain in earnings usually represents a two-part process.[6] First, the change in earnings of trainees is measured as the difference between earnings in some specified period after training compared to before training. Second, to assess the gain in earnings that can be credited to the training programs, the change in earnings for a trainee group is compared to a change in earnings of a control group, which did not receive government subsidized training. It is the difference between the changes that is denoted as the earnings gain from training; and it is this value that is netted against program costs. Some studies have also tried to measure the loss in earnings when a trainee was withdrawn from the labor market and placed in an institutional training program.[7] When the gain in earnings over the observed time period was not sufficient to cover program costs, authors have assumed that the gains would continue over a considerably longer period.[8] It is not atypical to find assumed five or ten year durations on earning gains that were observed over only one year.

Existing cost-benefit analyses may not have provided accurate information because they were performed under highly restrictive assumptions. They typically assumed that equal marginal value product, and, hence, gains in the earnings of trainees equal increments to aggregate consumption created by the programs. They use the dollar value of inputs to measure the consumption costs imposed on taxpayers through the programs without considering the equity costs from the transfer of benefits to shareholders. If the discounted gains in earnings exceed discounted program costs, the studies argue both that the programs are efficient and that they are distributing sufficient benefits to trainees to more than offset costs to taxpayers. These studies simply overlook the existence of specific skills and consider only wages determined in a manner consistent with simple neoclassical price theory.

Chapter 1 presented the argument that a much more reasonable supposition for an analysis of manpower programs is that they are a government purchase of entry port jobs in private industry for persons in specified socioeconomic circumstances. A firm sells its available jobs because it is profitable. But such a sale may not be efficient from a social point of view. If any job a firm is selling has a given wage tied to it and not to the productivity of the trainee, then the wage gains to the trainee may not be a function of his increased productivity. Rather such wage gains are a function of the jobs that administrators are prepared to purchase, either directly through on-the-job training or indirectly through institutional training. The trainee's productivity may be increased through the training that is in the purchase, but it need not increase. Whether it does or not and whether any increase is sufficient to offset the costs of the program is an empirical question. But that question cannot be answered by assuming a strict relationship between wages and productivity.

If one views a manpower program as a purchase agreement, then this leads to another question about its impact. To what extent are those firms that would have hired disadvantaged persons without subsidies selling jobs that, in effect, they would have been prepared to give away? A study that does not ask this question cannot provide meaningful results. One cannot answer that question by calculating wage changes or wage gains measured against a control group. One must investigate the firms that have been hiring trainees.

Reinterpretation of the Results of Manpower Program Studies

Studies of manpower programs often contain a common methodological short-coming. They do not provide direct information about the reasons firms decide either to hire the graduates of institutional manpower programs or contract for on-the-job training programs. A critical review suggests they overestimated the benefits for trainees and that an accurate estimate would require data about the hiring firms.

The Somers and Stromsdorfer study of manpower programs in West Virginia, which concluded that the training was socially desirable, did qualify its judgments. The impact of the programs may have been largely a substitution of persons processed through the programs for both similar but untrained persons and other more qualified who would have been hired in the absence of the subsidized programs. To the extent that the programs substituted one group of young and usually unemployed persons for another, the total benefits of the program accruing to the young and unemployed must be reduced. If more normally acceptable employees were also displaced and subsequently had difficulty finding employment, the net social benefits of the programs were overestimated. This is particularly significant in a depressed area where job possibilities are scarce.

Of course Somers and Stromsdorfer were aware of these problems. Somers,[9] in his separate discussion of the West Virginia survey, admitted that "many employers are induced to hire trainees not because of the skill acquired in their training, but because of the other gains associated with the training program. They feel that the trainees have been carefully screened, tested, and interviewed in the selection process." This, in itself, suggests that the substitution of trained for untrained hires may have been substantial. Besides, why devote resources to training, if the acquired skills did not, in themselves, generate employment opportunities?

One could reasonably speculate that Somers was concerned about the magnitude of the substitution. This is indicated by his weak defense of the possibility that subsidized retraining created additional jobs for persons considered in need of employment. He writes,

In some cases, *it is hoped, the employer might* [my emphasis] be induced to establish a job in order to take advantage of the subsidized skill now made available to him. . . . It is only under such circumstances that we can be certain that the worker's increased productivity has created a job for the unemployed instead of another.[10]

But an estimate of the number of new jobs created by the program requires a study of firms.[11] Besides, the profit incentive outlined in Chapter 1 suggests that firms might substitute subsidized persons for the least desirable among the non-subsidized that would have been hired.

Somers and Stromsdorfer are not alone in asserting that manpower programs have been in general socially desirable. Borus also argues that subsidized training has had a significant impact on the earnings of trainees. He divides his sample into six groups: workers who withdrew from retraining and did not use it, workers who withdrew from retraining without employment, workers who refused retraining for employment, workers who refused retraining without employment, workers who withdrew from retraining for employment, and workers who completed and used their retraining.

Applying multiple regression techniques, Borus corrects for the varying socioeconomic characteristics of the trainees.[12] He calculates that workers who completed and used their training averaged per week $7.44 more than workers who completed but did not use their training, $8.83 more than workers who refused training without employment, and $15.06 more than workers who withdrew from training without employment. However, in a footnote, Borus mentions that persons who withdrew from training for employment earned $4.03 and persons who refused training for employment earned $10.56 per week more than those who completed and used their training.[13] Borus also reports that persons in all groups earned about $2.00 per hour. Differences in earnings, "were attributed more to lower unemployment than to higher wage rates."[14]

Borus overlooks essential information by comparing the benefits of training against only persons who were unemployed when they left the program, while excluding those whose initial alternative to training was employment. This procedure overstates the benefits of training. Those who refused or quit training probably did not receive the benefits of the placement services generally associated with training programs. Consequently, the benefits from training may have been only rapid placement on a first job and therefore of a very short run. This is indicated by the observations that wage rates were not affected by subsidized training and that persons whose immediate alternative to training was employment actually earned more than trainees. If a rapid placement service for the unemployed represented the principal benefit to the trainees, Borus' assumed ten-year run on benefits estimated over only the first year after training is grossly overoptimistic. More important, if rapid placement was the principal cause of the observed differences in earnings, then Borus ignores the essential question. Were the training subsidies necessary for persons to acquire their subsequent employment? Once again, data on firms are essential for an answer to this question and consequently essential for a reliable estimate of benefits from training expenditures.

In another study Hardin and Borus sampled people in Michigan over 1962-1964 who received training in occupations commonly included in training programs throughout the nation. The sample was drawn from a variety of programs, with a separate control group for each program in the study. Structuring the study in this way is desirable. It allows comparisons of the effect on earnings between varying amounts of subsidized training offered in different programs and whatever amounts of training the control groups could acquire for themselves through the informal training activities usually associated with any job opportunity. For example, their sample includes some persons who received sixty hours of training as arc welders, while elsewhere in the state others received over two hundred hours. Thus, if a program began at time zero and ended at time H, earnings increase for both the trainee and control group were measured as earnings over period H to H plus one year minus earnings over the period from zero minus one year to zero.

One should emphasize that the formal training programs do not compete merely with alternatives of unemployment or low wage employment. Such programs must also compete with available informal training opportunities. That such opportunities exist, even for persons eligible for training under ARA and MDTA, is attested to by the mean increment to annual earnings of $1,308 for the control groups. This increment to earnings is compared to a mean increment of $1,524 for the experimental groups of trainees. Since the standard deviation in increments to annual earnings was $2,050, the obvious conclusion is that formal subsidized training had no statistically significant effect on earnings. Hardin and Borus argue that a simple t test on incremental earnings caused by subsidized training may overlook the impact of other significant variables; and thus multivariate analysis may still prove that the formal subsidized training had a statistically significant impact.[15] Of course, if the groups that Hardin and Borus labeled as "control" represent true control groups, multivariate analysis would add no new information about the impact of training subsidies.

After a number of intermediate regressions, Hardin and Borus present a final regression in which formal training is omitted because it has been statistically very insignificant through intermediate regressions. But this final regression contains a curious but statistically significant variable upon which they base both conclusions and policy recommendations. The results obtained from this variable are summarized in Table 2-1.

The numerator of the variable represents a 1,-1 code, where persons who received subsidized training were assigned a 1. H is the number of hours of training scheduled in a manpower program. Since a trainee and a control group were determined for each sampled program and the hours of scheduled training varied among programs, (Training Status)/H^2 was intended to measure the effect on earnings of varying amounts of subsidized training. The coefficient of regression on this variable was positive and significant. Thus, Hardin and Borus conclude that short training programs, because they generate a larger post-training increment in earnings, may be preferable to long programs.[16]

Table 2-1
Impact of the Duration of Formal Training

Variable	Coefficient of Regression	Standard Error	Significance Level
(Training Status)/H^2	13,515,534.880	4,474,804.611	.01

Source: U.S., Office of Manpower Policy, Evaluation, and Research, *Economic Benefits and Costs of Retraining Courses in Michigan*, by Einar Hardin and Micheal E. Borus (Washington, D.C.: Government Printing Office, 1969).

This surprising conclusion is certainly subject to critical review. Fortunately, Borus and Hardin present enough information to facilitate such a review, and their study will be criticized on two grounds. First, assuming that their results are accurate, contrary to their conclusion, many manpower programs may not have been socially desirable because they created few if any benefits for a substantial proportion of persons receiving such training. Second, a positive and significant coefficient for (Training Status)/H^2 represents an illogical result. Any implied increment benefits from short training programs can be explained away with a more logical argument than those that Borus and Hardin presented to defend their results.

Retraining taken as a whole probably did not represent a good investment for society. Hardin and Borus's cost-benefit ratios suggest this. Their results are reproduced in Table 2-2. For all programs over 200 hours, the cost-benefit ratios were negative. Eighty percent of all sampled programs lasted 200 or more hours. Thus the cost-benefit ratios for the sample taken as a whole were extremely small, and were less than one when the duration of such benefits was assumed to be five years. More important these small cost-benefit ratios are probably overestimated. They were calculated using (Training Status)/H^2 to estimate benefits to the trainees. But this variable implies illogical conclusions.

A positive coefficient on (Training Status)/H^2 implies Figure 2-1. In the

Table 2-2
Benefits and Costs of Retraining Sample of 503 Trainees

| | | Whole Sample | By Hours of Training | | | |
			60-200	201-600	601-1200	1201-1920
Annual Benefits		$ 251	976	−5	−121	−136
Total Costs		$1261	346	885	2183	3293
Benefit/Cost Ratios						
Service Life	Discount Rate					
5 years	5%	.85	12.22	*	*	*
	10%	.75	10.70	*	*	*
10 years	5%	1.52	21.79	*	*	*
	10%	1.21	17.34	*	*	*
15 years	5%	2.05	29.29	*	*	*
	10%	1.50	21.47	*	*	*

Source: U.S., Office of Manpower Policy, Evaluation, and Research, *Economic Benefits and Costs of Retraining Courses in Michigan*, by Einar Hardin and Micheal E. Borus (Washington, D.C., Government Printing Office, 1969).

Note: An abbreviated table that omits the breakdown of cost-benefit ratios by scheduled hours of training appears on page 279. The information that the ratios were negative for 200 or more hours of training can be taken from a preliminary draft, Chapter 9, page 9, or can be calculated from the results provided in Chapters 4-12 of the final draft.

*Indicates negative values

figure, G_T is the earnings increment from subsidized training, and G_T approaches infinity as H approaches zero and approaches zero as H approaches infinity. Thus a training program that schedules no training time offers the largest incremental benefits. A formal training program, on-the-job or out-of-plant, represents a training subsidy to firms that hire enrollees of such programs. In general, the longer the training program, the more funds that are expended for training resources, that is, the more training any individual receives. If earnings gains from shorter programs exceed gains from longer programs, this implies that firms have a relative preference for less well as opposed to better trained employees, that is, for smaller as opposed to larger subsidies.

Nevertheless, the variable was significant and this requires at least a tentative explanation. Hardin and Borus list the forty programs included in their sample, giving length of training courses, training occupations, and locality in which the course was given.[17] A careful examination of that list indicates that courses that taught the same skills varied considerably in length. For example, an arc welder course in Iron Mountain lasted six weeks, while one in Detroit lasted two weeks. This is not atypical. Three machine operator courses in the Port Huron area lasted four, six, and eight weeks, while machine operator courses in Benton Harbor and Flint lasted thirty-two and forty-two weeks.

Borus and Hardin's results indicate that persons who received the two-week welding course or the eight-week machine operator course would earn more after short training than those who received more training. This could occur if an expanding demand or limited supply of machine operators in Port Huron and of welders in Detroit resulted in relatively higher wages or more job security. Given

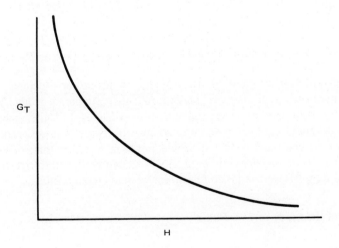

Figure 2-1. The Increment to Earnings of Trainees.

oquivalent supply and demand conditions throughout the state, one would logically expect the better trained to earn more than the more poorly trained. If demand conditions are not similar, then one would expect shorter courses to be established in areas where the excess demand for a given skill is acute. In such areas, persons receiving even limited training may be readily marketable. But this does not imply that shorter courses yield benefits in excess of longer courses. It may imply merely that the more scarce the skill, the greater the benefits of employment.

One could argue that trainees who could acquire such profitable employment at a small cost may have been in a relatively favorable position to acquire such employment without training subsidies. Recalling the arguments of the previous chapter, we can say that firms that would hire such persons in the absence of subsidies could profitably offer a substantial number of job openings in exchange for relatively small subsidy payments. Thus, the wage benefits to the trainees are not solely a function of the training program but are founded in part on employment opportunities that existed with or without subsidies. But once again an assessment of the employment opportunities that existed without subsidized training programs requires an analysis of the firms that hired persons who received subsidized training.

Many cost-benefit studies, such as those of Borus, Somers, and Somers and Stromsdorfer, contain biases that overestimate the benefits to trainees. Re-examination of the Hardin and Borus study, for example, shows that its most significant results may have been disregarded, the statistically insignificant difference in the gain in mean annual earnings between trainee and control groups, and the negative benefits from 80 percent of the programs. Since Borus, Somers, and Somers and Stromsdorfer noted that subsidized training did not affect hourly wages, and since the Borus and Hardin study indicates that subsidized training did not measurably affect earnings when measured against control groups, the subsidy programs may, in fact, have principally benefited firms.

To provide information about the effect of manpower programs and elim-inate the biases that may be present in other studies, a study should be consistent with the theoretical arguments in Chapter 1. Unlike many other studies it should consider that subsidies may be larger than necessary to gain employment for trainees, and it should not assume either that increments in earnings measure increments in productivity caused by the subsidized training or that the subsidies were required to gain subsequent employment.

Design of the Study of Two Firms

Objectives

To provide a better assessment than in many previous studies of the magnitude and distribution of program benefits, the empirical study in the following chapters will investigate the experience of two establishments in their hiring and training under the inducement of subsidy payments. This allows an analysis of variables, the reasons that the firms implemented manpower programs and the benefits they received to the exclusion of benefits to trainees, that could not be estimated without observations of the firms. Therefore the study should provide more information than has been available in many others.

Complete assessment of a project's social value would require evaluation of the direct and indirect consumption changes of all persons over time. In a manpower program this would include effects upon trainees, nontrainees, consumers, shareholders, and taxpayers. But this study will concentrate on the effects upon only trainees and indirectly on shareholders by estimating returns to the firms. Although this is unavoidable because of unavailable data, it is not a serious shortcoming because the trainees and the firms that hire them would be the most seriously affected by the manpower programs. A second limitation might be more serious. The study does not follow up on persons who quit the firm. If subsidized training was essential for the trainees to get work with the surveyed firms, and if the development and refinement of skills during that employment allowed them to find good jobs when they quit, then the earnings from the subsequent jobs should be included in the benefits of the program. On the other hand, we may conclude that the trainees could have been hired by the surveyed firms without subsidies. If we do, then their level of skill development may be a function of their employment rather than of the subsidies. Under this circumstance the absence of follow-up data would not affect estimates of the social value of the programs because their social value is net benefits as a function of subsidies.

To assess distribution effects, we will compare program costs to benefits for firms and for trainees. This requires a distinction between benefits of employment with the surveyed firms and the benefits or costs created by subsidy payments. This means that wage gains to subsidized persons similar in socioeconomic characteristics to other persons hired by the firm for the same jobs are highly suspect. While such wage gains result from employment with the subsidized firm, the subsidies may not have been required to create such employment. But even if subsidies did not create employment they may have increased productivity or reduced absenteeism and turnover. To the extent that such benefits were passed on to employees as higher wages or more rapid promotions, such benefits to employees must be credited to the subsidized programs.

First socioeconomic characteristics of sample populations of trainees will be contrasted with those of control groups. Persons in the control groups were hired into the same jobs over the same time periods as the sample of subsidized persons. Comparisons of subsidized and non-subsidized hires allows judgment of the extent to which the subsidies induced the firms to hire persons that they would not have accepted otherwise.

The studies will then consider the cost impact of subsidized training on the contracting firms. Three cost parameters will be analyzed in detail: turnover, absenteeism, and productivity. The incidence of such costs among the sample and control group population will first be related to socioeconomic variables including government subsidized training, and then, wherever possible, translated into dollar costs.

Considering the impact of the programs on the returns to the firm, subsidized employees may prove expensive to hire and train. But purchases of training resources with public funds may substitute for the normal costs incurred by firms when they hire and train. The cost savings from this substitution represents a return to the firm. This is simply a transfer payment between taxpayers and shareholders. Of course the firm may also receive additional benefits from the program because the job performance of the subsidized, measured by turnover, absenteeism, and productivity, may exceed normal performance. These returns represent efficiency benefits. But we must determine how often such benefits are passed on to employees as higher wages or more promotions, because if they are not passed on, they may accrue to the firm.

Cost and benefit measures are independent of a program's setting, on-the-job or institution. The relevant cost measures are the reduced efficiency if the firm lowers hiring standards and accepts unusually poor job performance and the opportunity cost of resources used in training only because of the subsidy program. The firm's benefits would result from reducing its training costs below normal. The employees receive benefits if the subsidy program gets them previously unattainable entry port jobs or promotions.

Surveyed Firms

The first firm to be discussed is a shipbuilding company. The skills it required as inputs—welding, shipfitting, pipefitting, and sheetmetal work—are general in that they are in demand in the labor market external to the firm. This is indicated by the fact that hires were placed at the appropriate step on a nine-rung wage ladder in their respective skills. This ladder begins at unskilled third class and ends at skilled first class. Denoting someone is an unskilled welder or pipefitter provides the firm with the flexibility it requires to hire and train persons who have little or no experience in the required skills.

Subsidized manpower programs were not the shipbuilder's first experience in training unskilled hires. Before the firm contracted for formal on-the-job training subsidies, it had established informal training for unskilled hires. For most skills, new men were immediately assigned to an experienced employee at a work station, where he and the station's supervisor would share the training burden. Only welders were not immediately assigned to the work area because they first were required to reach a specified proficiency. Therefore the firm had formal vestibule welding training that lasted an average of six weeks for those without experience. This took place in a plant area reserved for training. After vestibule training welders were assigned to work stations where a skilled employee and the station supervisor continued their training.

Between early 1965 and 1967, the firm contracted for several on-the-job training programs which consisted of one instructor who assumed all training responsibilities for ten new employees during 26-week subsidized training courses in welding, shipfitting, pipefitting, and sheetmetal work. Instructors, who had been skilled employees and supervisors on the shipbuilder's payroll, were relieved of their usual responsibilities and their salaries were paid with federal funds. The trainees were selected by the firm at its hiring window. In other words, they were drawn from the firm's normal pool of job applicants.

Along with trainees, instructors were assigned to work stations. Only the subsidized welding programs, because of the requirement of a minimum standard, contained six weeks of vestibule training, with instructor's salaries and material and equipment costs all subsidized. This training was identical to the firm's vestibule training before subsidy programs. It used the same instructors and the same area of the plant that had always been reserved for the vestibule training of welders. After the welders in the subsidized programs completed vestibule training, they were assigned like other skills to an instructor for twenty weeks of subsidized on-the-job training.

The second establishment manufactures electronic components. Unlike the shipbuilder, where all trainees were men, this firm trained both men and women. No person in either the trainee or comparison groups listed on their application forms previous employment in jobs like those assigned by the firm. This could result because either very few firms in the area used the same skills needed by the components manufacturer or it did not pay wages high enough to attract previously experienced job applicants. Whatever the cause, the absence of skilled job applicants may be constrasted to the shipbuilder, where a wide range of manufacturers, body shops, and construction, plumbing, or roofing contractors need the same skills, and a substantial proportion of job applicants indicated previous experience in these skills.

The difference in the frequency of skilled persons applying to the two firms is reflected in a comparison of their wage and job assignment practices. For example, the shipbuilder would assign a starting wage to a welder on the basis of his previous experience. The wage was associated with a skill rating and ideally the skill rating determined the tasks that a person was assigned to perform. Although this was the norm, pressures caused by inadequate numbers of highly skilled employees, the need for a larger labor force, and high rates of absenteeism forced some deviation from it. But the norm was that previous experience determined the skill rating, which in turn determined wage and job, defined as a mix of tasks assigned to persons with the same skill rating. In contrast, the electronics manufacturer would assign a starting wage solely on the basis of an employee's job title. Thus women hired as "mechanical assemblers" were offered a wage specific to the title and to the production department to which they were assigned. For the jobs in the survey, the assignments were mostly a function of the location of the most serious need for additional labor rather than the previous experience of an applicant.

Since the skills required by the components manufacturer appeared to be specific, it had to train everyone it hired for the jobs included in this survey. As with the shipbuilder, this firm used informal training on-the-job before it had a subsidized program. In early 1970 it used federal funds to establish a vestibule training program for both job orientation and skill development in the assembly of computer components. The subsidized vestibule training occurred in a separate area within the plant and before assignment in normal work areas. One feature of this program was similar to the shipbuilder's. It used the firm's skilled employees and supervisors as subsidized training inputs. But it differed from the shipbuilder's program in two important ways. First the trainees were not selected from the firm's normal applicant pool, but were referred to it from community employment centers of the local Concentrated Employment Program contractor. Second, the component manufacturer's program was an employment opportunity in addition to the opportunity provided by a job vacancy within a production department. By beginning training before a job vacancy appeared, its program necessarily created income during vestibule training. After this, trainees were transferred to production, where training continued with informal instruction from supervisors.

Multivariate Analysis

The objective of the multivariate analysis is to test whether subsidized training had an independent impact on cost parameters such as absenteeism, turnover, and productivity. Since we neither assume that wages equal marginal value product, nor that subsidies reflect the true costs to the firm of hiring subsidized employees, measurement of differences in length of service, productivity, and absenteeism caused by formal subsidized training are central to an assessment of the costs and benefits of such programs. Whether the firms did or did not lower their hiring standards, what impact did the subsidized programs have on the cost parameters? We will first assess the impact of socioeconomic variables, including subsidized training. We will then be able to estimate differences in return streams among groups of subsidized and non-subsidized hires. This will facilitate a more perceptive understanding of the factors that motivated the firms to hire subsidized labor.

Hiring Criteria and Socioeconomic Characteristics of
Employees

It is assumed that for any job at any point in time a firm has minimum hiring standards in terms of socioeconomic characteristics such as age, sex, or years of education. It is also assumed that information collected on the firm's application forms is relevant to their hiring decisions. Thus, if a control group and trainee group are similar in those socioeconomic characteristics listed on such forms, then one may reasonably conclude that the trainee group would be eligible for employment without subsidized training.

The firms may use subjective as well as objective criteria in their hiring decisions. These cannot be captured by the firm's application forms, because they represent the response of an interviewer. But if a firm applies different hiring standards to control and trainee groups, whether those standards are objective or subjective, then one would not expect the two groups to be similar in variables such as percentage of a sample population that is black or percentage seeking a first job. Unless one is prepared to argue that the subjective impression that a person makes is completely independent of the socioeconomic variables that characterize him, then any observation that the sample population of trainees is identical to a control group is strong evidence that the trainee group could have satisfied the hiring criteria applied to the control group.

The trainee group may differ from the control group. Presumably, the firms use socioeconomic variables as an indicator of the job performance that can be expected from any applicant. If a firm does lower its hiring criteria, then we must develop estimates of the cost, both in the returns to the firm and in reduced economic efficiency, which are imposed when a firm employs subsidized trainees. This is essential in assessing the independent impact of the training resources that are purchased because of the subsidy program. Thus, multivariate analysis must be applied to estimate both the costs imposed on the firm as it lowers hiring standards and the benefits generated by subsidized training. These benefits are the improved job performance that are directly attributable to that training.

Estimation Technique

The multivariate analyses will regress variables measuring length of service and absenteeism on the socioeconomic characteristics listed on that firm's application forms as well as a 0,1 dummy that indicates subsidized training. Such data, however present problems because one can reasonably expect strong colinearity among explanatory variables such as age and years in the labor force.

It is impossible to determine the independent impact of a highly colinear variable. Principal components analysis, discussed in detail in the appendix, allows us to identify sets of colinear variables that have had significant impacts on cost parameters. This is sufficient for our study. We are not interested in predicting the incidence and magnitude of turnover and absenteeism problems among the sample population because we are not interested in predicting the income redistribution and efficiency impacts of subsidized training programs undertaken by the firm. We are interested in measuring the distributional and efficiency impacts that the programs have already caused. Furthermore, we do not need to know whether a year of additional education reduced absenteeism by 0 percent, 1 percent, or 5 percent. We are mostly interested in whether years of education had a statistically significant impact. This is sufficient to indicate that the sample population was not truly homogeneous in job performance. It is then a simple matter to divide the sample population into subgroups based on education and calculate the extent to which labor costs varied among or between such subgroups. Calculating such variations represents one of the purposes of the statistical analysis, because although labor costs may vary among subgroups, subsidy payments did not. Thus the statistical analysis reveals distributional impacts of the programs that would not have been otherwise apparent.

Subsidized training is the only variable for which a precise estimate of its independent impact truly interests us. We can only hope that this variable is not strongly colinear with other explanatory variables, or if it is, that the entire set of variables colinear with subsidized training had no measurable impact on length of service, absenteeism, or productivity.

Productivity presents an additional problem. Along with any socioeconomic variables that may be relevant, it was argued in Chapter 1 that productivity at any point in time is a function of a person's skills when he enters production as well as subsequent training. Although it may be possible to list the amounts of some of the training resources of formal subsidized training, in general, it is impossible to measure precisely informal training resource purchased for the control group, because we do not know how supervisors and skilled employees divided their work day between their training and production responsibilities. We can, however, use a variable t, which measures weeks spent in production as a proxy for the amount of training resources purchased up to and including a given week. We can also use a dummy variable as a proxy for the different amounts of various training resources purchased for individuals in either the trainee or control groups. This variable is denoted by (xt) where

(2.1) $xt = 1$ for all persons in the control group; and

(2.2) $xt = t$ for all persons in the subsidized group.

We can then estimate a relationship

(2.3) $P_t = \alpha(t)^{\beta_1}(xt)^{\beta_2}$

In effect we are constructing a learning curve by estimating how productivity changes over time. We may assume that both the subsidized and control groups have the same intercept, which would be reasonable if we can argue that the two groups were equally proficient when placed in production. The variable (xt) facilitates a test on the shape of the learning curve. If β_2 is statistically significant, then $(\beta_1 + \beta_2)$ is the coefficient that would be used to estimate the productivity of members of the subsidized group at any point in time, while β_1 would be used for the control group.

If only the subsidized trainees received at least part of their training before being placed on a job, we would also wish to test whether such persons were more productive than a control group when they were first placed on a job. Thus we must test whether the intercept term, α, varied between the control and subsidized groups. This can be accomplished through the use of another dummy variable, where

(2.4) $x \equiv e$ for the trainee group, and

(2.5) $x \equiv 1$ for the control group.

The estimated relationship is

(2.6) $P_t = \alpha (t)^{\beta_1} (xt)^{\beta_2} (x)^{\beta_3}$.

Summary

Reliable estimates of costs and benefits require observations of the firms that hire manpower program trainees. To analyze the effects of programs used by two firms, we must structure control groups to parallel the trainee groups. These control groups will be comprised of persons hired to perform the same jobs as the trainees over those time periods when the trainees were being hired. If trainee and control groups are very similar, then this is strong evidence that the trainees were eligible for employment without subsidies.

Multivariate analysis will be applied by regressing measurable aspects of job performance on the socioeconomic characteristics of the sample populations. Obviously, these regressions are based on the assumption that since the firms bother to collect such information, it is relevant to their hiring decisions. If it is relevant to such decisions, then presumably some relationship does exist between socioeconomic characteristics and job performance.

Notes

1. Michael E. Borus, "A Benefit-Cost Analysis of Retraining the Unemployed," YALE ECONOMIC REVIEW 6 (Fall, 1964); 371-429.

2. Gerald Somers, "Retraining, an Evaluation of Gains and Costs," EMPLOYMENT POLICY AND THE LABOR MARKET, ed. by A.M. Ross (Berkeley: University of California Press, 1965), 271-298.

3. Gerald Somers and Ernst Stromsdorfer, "A Benefit-Cost Analysis of Manpower Retraining," INDUSTRIAL RELATIONS RESEARCH ASSOCIATION 17 (1964); 172-194.

4. U.S., Office of Manpower Policy, Evaluation, and Research, ECONOMIC BENEFITS AND COSTS OF RETRAINING COURSES IN MICHIGAN, by

Einar Hardin and Michael F. Borus (Washington, D.C.: Government Printing Office, 1969).

5. Thomas I. Ribich, EDUCATION AND POVERTY (Washington, D.C.: The Brookings Institute, 1968), 39-50, reviews the Borus and Somers and Stromsdorfer studies as well as some other benefit-cost studies of manpower programs. However, while the chapter in this book emphasizes the similarities among existing studies, Ribich emphasizes the dissimilarities. He argues that differences in benefit-cost ratios among such studies can, in part be traced to differences in assumptions made about the duration and magnitude of benefits and costs and about discount rates. For example, Somers and Stromsdorfer, "Manpower Training," 262-264, considers as benefits only the increment to earnings of trainees measured against a control group. Borus, "Retraining the Unemployed," 399, uses the total earnings of trainees. Ribich then asks the question: given the differing sets of assumptions that have been made, which one set is the most reasonable in analyses of manpower programs? The same question will be asked in this chapter; and the interested reader may consult Ribich to see for himself that the conclusions reached here are quite different from Ribich's.

6. See, for example, Somers and Stromsdorfer, "Manpower Retraining," as well as David A. Page, "Retraining Under the Manpower Development Act: A Cost-Benefit Analysis," PUBLIC POLICY 13 (1964); 262-264.

7. See, for example, Hardin and Borus, RETRAINING COURSES IN MICHIGAN.

8. See, for example, Borus and Hardin, RETRAINING COURSES IN MICHIGAN; and Michael Borus, John Brennan, and Sidney Rosen, "A Benefit-Cost Analysis of the Neighborhood Youth Corps: The Out-of-Plant Program in Indiana," JOURNAL OF HUMAN RESOURCES 5 (Spring, 1970); 139-159.

9. Somers, "Retraining, an Evaluation," 274.

10. Ibid.

11. Somers and Stromsdorfer, "Manpower Retraining," 184, argues that, "Even if it could be shown that retrained workers merely find employment that might otherwise go to the untrained, there are important political, economic, cultural, and social values in demonstrating that individual workers can gain through retraining." In rebuttal, there are more important political, economic, cultural, and social values in demonstrating that gains from subsidized training imposed a cost on nontrainees while yielding a consumption transfer from taxpayers to stockholders.

12. Borus, "Retraining the Unemployed," 379.

13. Ibid.

14. Ibid., 381.

15. Hardin and Borus, RETRAINING COURSES IN MICHIGAN, 96.

16. Ibid., 280.

17. Ibid., 70-72.

3 The Shipbuilder

Reviewing briefly what was discussed in Chapter 1, prospective employees were divided into groups on the basis of the job performance that they would yield if hired. It was argued that if a firm hired for an entry port job from a group in excess of the number who could be subsidized, then the subsidy program had no impact on employment for that group. In Chapter 2 it was argued that firms have two methods for screening prospective employees, objective criteria such as age or education and subjective criteria implicit in a job interview.[1] Although we can observe only objective criteria, we may argue that if two groups are identical in socioeconomic characteristics and both groups were hired into the same entry port jobs, then individuals in one group could have passed the hiring criteria applied to the other. Finally, it may be reasonably assumed that the firm's hiring criteria is based on a relationship between socioeconomic characteristics and job performance. If both groups are identical in socioeconomic characteristics, then with identical training we could assume that they would perform identically on any job. In other words, the two groups are the same. Under this circumstance, a manpower program for one of the two identical groups hired for the same job would be subsidizing only intramarginal employees.

The first question which should be answered about the shipbuilder's on-the-job (OJT) training program is simply this: could the subsidized trainees have gotten their jobs without the aid of subsidies? Whatever the answer to this question, estimates of the trainees' job performance will be an important part of the analysis. Whether the subsidies did or did not induce the firm to lower hiring standards, we still want to know about differences in job performance between subsidized employees' and the firm's normal supply to calculate the distribution and magnitude of program costs and benefits.

Comparison of Trainee and Control Groups

Table 3-1 gives mean value of the socioeconomic characteristics of a sample of subsidized on-the-job (OJT) trainees and a control group of workers trained without subsidies through the usual informal procedure established by the firm prior to its manpower contracts. The control group was structured to parallel the OJT group in entry port jobs. Two considerations were relevant to the construction of such a parallel. First, since the OJT group was taught several different skills, the control group was structured so that the percentage of

Table 3-1
Socioeconomic Characteristics of Subsidized On-the-Job Trainees

Variable	Subsidized On-the-Job Trainees N=200	Control Group N=100
Mean Age	24.49	24.67
Mean Years in Labor Force	4.72	4.97
Mean Years of Education	11.46	11.51
Mean Number of Dependents	.93	.89
Percentage Raised and Educated in the South	7.5%	8.0%
Percentage Non-White	4.5%	4%
Mean Hourly Wage on Previous Job	$2.167	$2.224
Mean Weeks on that Job	20.8	21.9
Mean Hourly Wage on Second Job Before Employment with the Surveyed Firm	$2.006	$2.007
Mean Weeks on that Job	18.6	17.4
Percentage Not in Labor Force Prior to Employment with the Surveyed Firm	19.0%	22.0%
Mean Weeks Unemployed the Year Before Employment with the Surveyed Firm	5.08	5.35
Mean Number of Jobs the Year Preceding Employment with the Surveyed Firm	1.73	1.81
Mean Starting Job with the Surveyed Firm	1.964	2.135

individuals in that group who received training in any one skill was equivalent to the percentage in the OJT group who received such training. Second, the control group was structured to be similar to their trainee group in their initial placement on the firm's nine-rung wage ladder. Thus the control group neither includes persons who were hired into the upper three classifications on the ladder nor does it include a random sample on non-subsidized persons who were hired into the unskilled or semi-skilled classifications. Rather the control group is structured to parallel the subsidized OJT group in wages at time of hire, and presumably, in skills when hired.

Most of the variables listed in Table 3-1 are self-explanatory. Only one requires explanation. This variable, "Mean Starting Job with the Surveyed Firm," is a dummy where workers hired as unskilled third class were assigned a value of 1 to indicate their place of entry on the wage ladder. Workers hired farther up the ladder were assigned progressively larger values, with skilled first class assigned a value of 9. The classification of unskilled third class is for persons with absolutely no experience in the required skills. But notice that the mean value for the variable was 1.964 for those in the OJT programs. In other words, the firm was using subsidies to train people who did have some previous experience in the required skills. In fact, 20 percent of the OJT sample had sufficient previous experience to be hired as semi-skilled employees (job classification 4 through 6) at hourly wages ranging from $2.63 to $2.89 in mid-1967.

A comparison of the subsidized and non-subsidized hires does suggest that the subsidized employees would have been eligible for employment without subsidies. Table 3-1 demonstrates that the differences in mean values of the socioeconomic characteristics between the two groups are statistically insignificant at the .05 level. The subsidized trainees were on average no younger, no more unstable on their previous jobs, no less well paid on these previous jobs, and no less educated than the control group. For example, Table 3-2 compares only those who were subsidized and hired as unskilled third class. Although unskilled third class hires are younger, less stable on previous jobs, and less well paid on those jobs when compared to the larger samples of OJT and control group persons drawn from all unskilled and semi-skilled classifications, the differences in mean values of the socioeconomic characteristics between subsidized and non-subsidized persons hired as unskilled third class are all statistically insignificant at the .05 level. The shipbuilder was prepared to hire without subsidies persons who had no previous experience in the required skills. These non-subsidized persons were, on average, identical to similarly unskilled subsidized persons in those socioeconomic variables listed on the firm's job application form.

This similarity between subsidized OJT and non-subsidized hires can be explained by the fact that the firm was allowed to use its own hiring window when selecting subsidized OJT trainees. Thus the population from which it selected such persons was the same as that from which it selected other non-subsidized unskilled and semi-skilled hires. The decision to place an unskilled hire in the subsidized formal OJT program was based largely on whether a vacancy was available in that program at the time of hire. Thus placement in the program was randomly distributed among one population of applicants who approached the firm with little or no experience in the required skills.

While the manpower programs were in progress, persons identical to those subsidized were hired into the same job classifications and informally trained to perform the same tasks as the subsidized trainees. That they performed the same tasks was confirmed by direct observation, which will be discussed in following sections of this chapter. If subsidized and non-subsidized persons are identical

Table 3-2

Socioeconomic Characteristics of OJT and Control Groups with no Previous Experience

Variable	Subsidized On-the-Job Employees N=84	Control Group N=42
Mean Age	21.87	21.79
Mean Years in the Labor Force	2.74	2.71
Mean Years of Education	11.5	11.7
Mean Number of Dependents	.64	.58
Percentage Raised and Educated in the South	8.1%	7.5%
Percentage Non-White	4.6%	2.5%
Mean Hourly Wage on Previous Job	$2.078	$2.091
Mean Weeks on that Job	16.5	17.2
Mean Hourly Wage on Second Job Before Employment with the Surveyed Firm	$1.972	$1.981
Mean Weeks on that Job	12.5	13.1
Percentage Not in Labor Force Prior to Employment with the Surveyed Firm	30.2%	35.0%
Mean Weeks Unemployed the Year Before Employment with the Surveyed Firm	6.3	6.5
Mean Number of Jobs the Year Preceding Employment with the Surveyed Firm	2.33	2.26
Mean Starting Job with the Surveyed Firm	1	1

and are performing the same tasks for the same pay, this suggests that the subsidized persons could have been employed by the firm without the aid of subsidies.

The Multivariate Analyses

While subsidized OJT training may not have increased the number of persons hired by the firm, it may have generated some benefits by inducing the purchase of additional training resources that may increase productivity or reduce turnover and absenteeism. The following section of this chapter will estimate the impact of subsidized training on the three cost parameters of absenteeism, turnover, and productivity. Observed differences in these parameters will, whenever possible, be translated into dollar values.

In assessing the impact of the OJT training on length of service and absenteeism, one may be tempted to argue that since the differences in the mean values of all socioeconomic characteristics between the control and OJT groups are statistically insignificant, then any statistically significant difference in the mean values for length of service or absenteeism could be attributed to the subsidized OJT training. Conversely, if the differences are statistically insignificant, one might conclude that the OJT training had no measurable impact on these cost parameters. In fact, this need not be true because, while mean values may be similar, the distributions around those means may be quite different. This becomes important if non-linear relationships are specified between dependent and some independent variables. For example, if one postulates that length of service is some function of the square root of years in the labor force, and the OJT group possesses a relatively larger percentage of the very young and very old, then one would expect the OJT group to average a shorter length of service when compared to the control group. The fact that they do not may be caused by subsidized OJT training. On the other hand, the OJT and control groups were drawn from the same applicant population. One would no more expect differences in the skews of socioeconomic characteristics than in their mean values.

Nevertheless, multivariate analysis will be applied. It may uncover a statistically significant impact for OJT training, but the expectation is that it will not. Multivariate analysis may, however, isolate other variables which are statistically significant. The assumption made in Chapter 1 that the subsidized population was homogeneous in expected job performance need not be true. For example, under the MA-3 program, those eligible for subsidies were "Poor persons who do not have suitable employment and who are either (1) school dropouts; (2) under twenty-two years of age; (3) forty-five years of age or older; (4) handicapped; or (5) subject to special obstacles to employment."[2] This definition has a serious shortcoming because while one is either covered by it or is not, homogeneously poor job performance should not be expected from such diversity of people. For the shipbuilder, the subsidy payment was independent of the job performance of each subsidized employee. If, in fact, job performances and costs varied among definable subgroups of the subsidized population, then one may conclude that the firm was receiving substantial benefits of transfer payments for that subset or subsets offering relatively good performance.

Regression Models

In specifying the regression equations the independent variables were taken from the application forms of the shipbuilder. Presumably the firm requests such

information because it indicates future job performance. It would seem therefore logical in specifying the regression models to assume that the firm knows
what it is doing when it asks for information from applicants. Table 3-3 lists the
independent variables, collected by the firm upon which the job performance
measures will be regressed. One variable in the table, job turnover rate, is a
transformation of data on the application form. It is the number of jobs divided
by years in the labor force. Presumably, this variable provides long-run
information about the tendency of employees to change jobs more or less
frequently.

Table 3-3
F **Tests on Each Independent Variable**

Variable	All OJT and Control	OJT and Control Hired as Unskilled Third Class
Age	78.49	22.21
Years in the Labor Force	72.79	27.19
Years of Education	3.92	2.86
Region Raised and Educated	4.63	4.42
Race	.82	1.29
Wage on Previous Job	5.40	7.14
Weeks Previous Job Held	4.17	5.19
Labor Force Status	4.17	5.19
Weeks Unemployed	5.39	8.42
Job Turnover Rate*	4.17	8.31
Starting Job	4.18	—
OJT	.90	1.01
Value of Determinant of the Correlation Matrix	.006	.008

*Job Turnover Rate is the number of jobs divided by years in the labor force.

Multicollinearity

Identifying the independent impact of many of the explanatory variables may be
impossible. The sample populations cause serious multicollinearity problems.
Table 3-3 gives the *F* tests for each variable when it is regressed on all other
explanatory variables. The table also gives the value of the determinant of the
correlation matrix. Examination of this table indicates the seriousness of the
multicollinearity problem. For example, consider the first column, which
includes all OJT trainees and all persons in the control group. The only variables

for which the F tests are statistically insignificant are race and subsidized OJT. All other F tests are statistically significant at the .01 level. The value of the determinant of the correlation matrix is .006. If one considers only those who were hired as unskilled third class and drops the variable indicating starting job classification, the multicollinearity problems diminish somewhat but remain serious. The multicollinearity stems essentially from missing observations. We simply do not have enough observations on persons who are twenty-five years of age and just entering the labor force.

In addition to race and OJT, labor force status is uncorrelated with other variables for the sample of only persons hired as unskilled third class. This variable is a 1,0 dummy where persons who have never previously held a job are coded as a zero. That this variable is uncorrelated with a variable such as years in the labor force is somewhat surprising. However, the homogeneously young sample population included persons who, for example, had a previous job but had been in the labor force considerably less than one year. They provided sufficient independent variation between labor force status and other explanatory variables to make the simple correlation coefficients between labor force status and each of the explanatory variables statistically insignificant at the .05 level for persons hired as unskilled third class.

Most important, OJT training does not offer any serious problems because the dummy variable used to indicate formal subsidized training was not colinear with any of the other socioeconomic characteristics that will be used as explanatory variables. Thus we can use ordinary least squares to attain an unbiased coefficient and reasonable t value for this variable. We can then proceed to principal component analysis as another technique to see if any other variables acting together had a statistically significant impact. The point to emphasize, however, is that ordinary least squares is sufficient to indicate the impact of OJT training.

Turnover

Turnover limits the length of the return stream that the firm realizes from any employee. Therefore the dependent variable is the length of service with the firm. This variable assumes a value from 1 to 130 weeks, the upper limit of observation on length of service. Table 3-4 presents the ordinary least squares estimates and the t tests both for the entire sample populations and for only those persons hired as unskilled third class. These coefficients are presented for a simple linear model. Various other combinations of linear and non-linear variables were also tried, but the results were no better and sometimes worse than those realized under the simple linear model.

All Skill Grades. Considering the first column of regression results, we find that starting job was significant at the .005 level. This variable measures experience in

Table 3-4

Coefficients of Regression with Length of Service as Dependent Variable

Variable	All OJT and Control Group N=300	Only OJT and Control Hired as Unskilled Third Class N=168	Variable	All OJT and Control Group N=168	Only OJT and Control Hired as Unskilled Third Class N=168
Age	.5013* (1.975)	.3105 (1.157)	Labor Force Status	6.441*** (2.763)	7.4315*** (4.021)
Years in the Labor Force	1.3057 (1.582)	.6321 (.9861)	Weeks Unemployed	−.4713 (1.036)	−.5713 (.938)
Years of Education	−.4832 (.969)	.1876 (.076)	Job Turnover Rate	−1.631 (1.428)	−.6205 (−.375)
Number of Dependents	1.3124 (.631)	1.6321 (1.208)	Starting Job	2.317*** (4.145)	− −
Region	−1.734 (−1.103)	−1.1315 (−.031)	OJT	.9176 (.874)	1.3176 (.625)
Race	−1.2038 (−.226)	.8762 (.115)	Intercept	15.6752	8.1348
Wage on Previous Job	3.376** (2.443)	2.8133* (1.753)	R^2	.1462	.1131
Weeks on that Job	.3815* (2.131)	.4618*** (3.047)	F	6.621	5.342

*Significant at .05
**Significant at .01
***Significant at .005

the required skills before employment with the surveyed firm. Thus persons who were more experienced and therefore more productive when hired also on average remained with the firm for a longer time. Of course, experienced employees also earned a higher starting wage. But the point to emphasize is that experienced and inexperienced hires varied in both the magnitude of costs, measured in part by wages and training costs, and the magnitude of benefits, measured as the value of their output over time.

Within limits, the manpower contract offered the same total subsidy payment to the firm regardless of the previous experience of the trainees. Obviously, limits did exist. Manpower program administrators would have objected if large numbers of highly skilled welders or pipefitters had received subsidized training. But within those limits, labor inputs offering different return streams were receiving the same subsidy payments.

Most important, on-the-job training did not affect the average length of the return streams. The variable OJT was very insignificant. Thus we can conclude that the subsidized training did not generate benefits by increasing an employee's length of service with the firm.

Unskilled Third Class. Considering only completely inexperienced hires, we find that once again, OJT was statistically insignificant and also that the population was by no means homogeneous in length of service. As the second column of Table 3-4 indicates, the coefficient on labor force status was positive and statistically significant. Persons who had previous work experience stayed with the firm longer. Two other variables, wage and months on previous job were also statistically significant. Thus even when one standardizes for previous experience in the required general skills, the population was not homogeneous in length of service, and OJT remained insignificant.

However, in contrast to the regression using the entire sample populations, when only the third class hires are considered, age is not statistically significant. The statistically significant impact of age for the entire sample population can be explained by the fact that age and starting job with the firm were highly correlated, and the regression coefficient on starting job was positive and significant at the .005 level. Thus age may be picking up the impact of previous experience; and when we standardize by considering only unskilled third class hires, the coefficient of age becomes statistically insignificant.

Principal component analysis was applied to isolate the independent dimensions among the colinear variables for the population of unskilled third class hires. This eliminates the multicollinearity problem, and subject to the restrictions discussed in the previous section and in the appendix, one can check the statistical significance of the colinear variables. The first four components explained 85 percent of the variation in all nine original colinear variables. None of the remaining five explained over 4 percent and were consequently omitted from further consideration.

Identifying the first four principal components, Table 3-5 gives the simple

Table 3-5
Correlation Coefficients

Variable Description	1	Component Numbers 2	3	4
Age	.913	−.136	.213	.121
Years in the Labor Force	.837	−.221	−.081	.038
Years of Education	−.435	−.071	.023	.754
Number of Dependents	.862	.360	−.072	−.229
Region	−.364	.050	−.278	.621
Wage on Previous Job	.335	.537	.868	.165
Weeks on that Job	.429	.217	.811	.183
Weeks Unemployed	.200	.927	−.021	−.002
Job Turnover Rate	−.297	.841	.225	.058
Latent Roots	3.023	2.106	1.551	1.071

corrolation coefficients between the components and the original variables. Component (1) is highly correlated with age, years in the labor force, and number of dependents. Thus this component is highly correlated with those variables which suggest maturity. Presumably, maturity results in preferences for stable employment and income and job security.

Component (2) is highly correlated with weeks of unemployment and job turnover rate. Large values for both variables indicate substantial previous turnover because more frequent turnover causes more frictional unemployment. Thus one would expect the two variables to be highly correlated. The simple correlation coefficient between them is significant at the .01 level.

Component (3) is highly correlated with the variables wage on last job before employment with the subsidized firm and weeks on that job. One could argue that this component reflects the impact on the wage rate on length of time that a job was held. On the other hand, the wage is certainly a function of the length of time that a person has held a job, because he receives standardized pay increases. Besides, the sample population did not show much variation in the wages on their last job. Sixty percent of those who held previous jobs earned between $1.75 and $2.05 per hour. Furthermore, the sample is comprised almost entirely of single young men. Those who had been working were typically stockboys, janitors, low wage factory workers, and construction laborers, jobs that offered some combination of low wages and unpleasant working conditions. One must wonder whether the difference between $1.80 and $2.00 per hour would have a measurable impact on the decisions of such persons to either keep or quit such jobs. Identifying, or in other words labeling, a component is admittedly subjective. But component (3) is assumed to reflect a preference for stable employment that is independent of working conditions and wages.

Component (4) is closely correlated with the variables years of formal education and region where raised and educated, which is a north-south dummy. Since the simple correlation coefficient between the two variables is significant at the .005 level, component (4) is assumed to reflect both the quality and quantity of formal education.

Table 3-6 gives the coefficients and t tests for a regression using the four components, and the dummy variables indicating OJT, race, and labor force status. Not surprisingly, the one component whose coefficient is statistically significant is highly correlated with two of the original variables whose coefficients were statistically significant under ordinary least squares. Thus, component (3) is significant at the .005 level. Persons who had recently revealed a relative preference for stable employment were more likely to be long-term employees if hired by the shipbuilders. Other than that, the coefficient on labor force status remained significant, the coefficient on OJT and race remained statistically insignificant; and coefficients on the other three components, which were highly correlated with variables whose ordinary least squares coefficients were insignificant, were also insignificant. Principal components analysis did not

Table 3-6
Coefficients for the Principal Components Regression

Independent Variable	Coefficient
Component (1)	4.36
	(1.315)
Component (2)	−.52
	(−.197)
Component (3)	7.312*
	(4.631)
Component (4)	1.74
	(.882)
Race	.8314
	(.103)
Labor Force Status	7.0123*
	(3.861)
OJT	1.4138
	(.602)
F Test on all Independent Variables	4.821*

*Significant at .005 level

add any new results. The 126 observations were sufficient to generate both enough independent variation among variables and enough rounding error so that the t tests on ordinary least squares estimates were reasonable even for highly colinear variables.

The important points to emphasize are these: first, the coefficient on OJT was very insignificant; and second, even when we standardize for previous experience in the required skills, we find three distinct groups with regard to the length of service that the firm can expect from any hire. These are: persons with previous relatively stable employment; those with previous unstable employment; and those with no previous work experience. Table 3-7 compares mean length of service for unskilled third class hires classified by age and previous job stability. Table 3-8 compares retention rates at 30 and 130 weeks for employees classified by previous job stability. These tables indicate the variation in length of service among definable subgroups of the control and OJT populations. Furthermore, as the multivariate analysis indicates, formal subsidized training did not reduce turnover costs among any of these subgroups by lengthening their term of employment.

Absenteeism

The absent employee imposes costs in two ways. First, the absence denies the firm his productive service. Second, the absent employee may reduce the productivity of his fellow employees.

Table 3-7
Length of Service (Sample of 50)

	Mean Age	Mean Weeks with Firm	Mean Months Previous Job
Unskilled Third Class by Age			
(1) Less than 25 with work experience	20.00	46	12.41
(2) Over 25	28.21	50	16.11
(3) Less than 25 with no work experience	20.33	23	—
Unskilled Third Class by Previous Job Stability			
(1) Ten or more months on previous job	22.97	76.50	25.47
(2) Less than ten months on previous job	22.08	31.17	4.11
(3) No Previous Job	20.33	23.00	—

Table 3-8
Percentage of Laborers Retained (Sample of 50)

	Retained After 30 Weeks	Retained at 130 Weeks
Previously Stable (more than ten months on previous job)*	52%	28%
Previously Unstable	45%	19%
Just Entering Labor Market	27%	8%

*Ten months is arbitrary. It was selected simply because 50 percent of the total sample fell below that specified length of previous service.

In specifying the regression equation, the dependent variable was the attendance rate. This variable was the ratio of total hours in attendance to the sum of total hours in attendance plus hours absent and tardy. The simple correlation coefficients between this and other variables, such as length of service or starting job classification, were insignificant. Comparing the mean value of the attendance rate for unskilled hires to those hired as semi-skilled third class, these values are .917 and .928. The standard deviation for the entire OJT and control group samples was .2808. The difference in mean values is highly insignificant. The difference in mean values between the OJT and control samples was .004 and also very insignificant.

Using multivariate analysis, both the ordinary least squares and the principal components regressions indicated that the independent variables did not explain the incidence of absenteeism. All independent variables and all components were very insignificant in all regressions on absenteeism. The F tests on the impact of the set of independent variables were generally less than .5. Thus the socioeconomic characteristics collected by the firm on its application blanks gave no clue as to who was likely to present costly problems of absenteeism. Furthermore, formal subsidized OJT training had no measurable impact on increasing the attendance rate.

Productivity

Restrictions on the availability of data limit the analysis to one common task in the plant for one skill, welding. Productivity was measured as the ratio of actual man hours of labor input to hours budgeted by the firm's cost accounting department. In specifying the regression, factors such as age, years in the labor force, and years of education were omitted, partly because supervisory personnel argued from experience that these variables did not affect productivity. They believed that a persons's general skills at time of hire and his subsequent training determined his productivity. This seems reasonable for manual skills such as welding, and available data on welders does confirm their observations. Since welders are required to reach a given level of proficiency before they are allowed to enter production, persons with no previous experience, those hired as unskilled third class, are required to undergo vestibule training for about six weeks. Since the OJT and control groups received identical vestibule training, the two groups took on average the same amount of time to acquire the skills necessary to enter production.

Table 3-9 compares selected socioeconomic characteristics for the six slowest and six fastest learners in vestibule training for both the OJT and control groups.

Table 3-9
Socioeconomic Characteristics of Fast and Slow Learners

Variables	OJT Group		Control Group	
	Six Slowest Learners	Six Fastest Learners	Six Slowest Learners	Six Fastest Learners
Mean Age	21.50	21.83	22.00	21.33
Mean Years of Education	12.00	11.70	11.70	11.33
Mean Weeks Unemployed	6.00	5.66	5.67	6.67
Mean Weeks on Previous Job	15.50	19.00	17.33	16.25
Mean Wage on that Job	$1.93	$1.98	$1.95	$2.00
Number with no Previous Work Experience	1	2	3	2

In other words, these are the twelve persons from each group who took the longest and the shortest time before being placed in production. The table indicates that mean values for these variables did not differ significantly between slow and fast learners. Consequently, productivity at any point in time is specified to be a function of general skills at the time of hire and training resources invested in the employee. We can standardize for entry level skills by considering only unskilled third class hires and estimate the productivity curve.

$$(3.1) \qquad P_t = \alpha(t)^{\beta_1} (xt)^{\beta_2}.$$

As discussed in the preceding chapter, this equation assumes that the intercept is the same for both the trainee and control groups and uses (xt) to determine if the slope of the productivity curve varies between the groups. Since vestibule training standardizes for skills when a person is placed on the job, it is logical to assume that the intercept term would not vary between the groups and that subsidized on-the-job training could affect only the slope.

In order to protect the firm's interests, the regression coefficients cannot be given because they would express actual productivity relative to the firm's labor standards, Table 3-10 gives only the t tests and the R^2. The t test on (xt) is insignificant. Thus, formal subsidized on-the-job training did not appear to increase learning rates and consequently did not increase productivity in the welding job at any point in time. This is not surprising. The programs covered the costs of some resources such as the salaries of on-the-job training instructors. These instructors substituted directly for experienced employees and supervisors who otherwise would have provided training. The full costs of any other training resources required to improve productivity would have been born by the firm. Thus the firm was not induced by the subsidy program to purchase the resources that might have improved the productivity of subsidized as opposed to non-subsidized hires.

Table 3-10
Regression of Productivity

Independent Variables	t Values
Intercept	3.707
t	−3.228
(xt)	.694
R^2	.494
F	138.631

Program Benefits

Benefits for the Firm

The shipbuilder's contracting for manpower programs that did not improve trainees' job performance may seem surprising, but when one considers the firm's motivations, it is not. Over the period covered by the surveyed programs, the firm increased its labor force from 3,000 to 5,000 despite a retention rate after thirty weeks of only 37.5 percent for unskilled third class hires. The firm correctly anticipated a growing training burden because it could not acquire all the skilled and semi-skilled hires it wished at existing wage rates; it had contract commitments with penalties for late deliveries; it had substantial excess plant capacity; and consequently it energetically pursued new contracts. In fact, management personnel concerned with production indicated that the capacity of the firm to use informal training was about exhausted. By late 1968, the firm was beginning to use formal training instructors for some of its non-subsidized unskilled hires.

These facts suggest that the efficiency effects for both the firm and the economy may have been insignificant. The programs neither created efficiency benefits through improved job performance nor introduced efficiency costs by requiring the firm to choose an inferior training method. It may have been forced to use formal training instructors whether their salaries were or were not subsidized.

Although the firm did not receive benefits by improving job performance, it did benefit by reducing its training costs. It was concerned mostly with establishing a program that would successfully integrate new workers into the job structure of the plant at a cost acceptable to the agency responsible for approving the subsidy payments. This does not mean that management was unaware of the possibility of larger subsidy payments. A representative of the firm testified before a congressional subcommittee that given the job performance of persons hired under the subsidy program, the firm doubted the subsidy to be adequate compensation. Thus, while the firm would certainly have preferred larger subsidy payments and larger contracts, its first concern was compensation for the costs it would have been forced to bear to provide the training necessary to generate acceptable performance by its unskilled hires.

Benefits for Employees

Subsidized training did not provide any measurable benefits for employees. Neither hiring nor promotion decisions were affected. The correlation coefficient between promotion rate and OJT is .058 and very insignificant. Furthermore, since the OJT trainees were no more productive than other unskilled hires, the subsidized training did not alter their marketable skills, which presumably might have affected their wages after they left the firm.

The next section of this chapter will use the information on the three cost parameters to present further arguments that dismiss the possibility that the subsidy increased the total employment of eligible persons. It will be demonstrated that the subsidy payments represented little more than a simple transfer in favor of shareholders.

Input Constraints

The subsidized program did not affect the job performance of the resource input that is denoted as unskilled third class welders. With or without subsidies, productivity, absenteeism, and length of service were unaffected. The manpower program lowered the price to the firm of resources such as unskilled third class welders. However, we will demonstrate that given its wage levels, the firm must have faced binding constraints on new employees with at least some experience in the required skills. Thus the cost of completing a surveyed task is greater if unskilled third class hires are used instead of unskilled second class hires. If the firm faced no constraints, we would expect it to adjust to one of two alternatives, either the cost of performing the task is the same whether by unskilled third class or unskilled second class hires, or one of the inputs would dominate, that is for example, the firm would hire only persons qualified as unskilled second class to perform the surveyed task and others similar to it. On the other hand, if unskilled third class hires represent a relatively more expensive input for the surveyed task, then this does substantiate the firm's own admission that inputs of more skilled persons were constrained. Many persons hired as unskilled second class were also included under the subsidy program. If inputs of such persons were constrained, subsidizing their training costs could have had no other impact than to transfer income from taxpayers to the firm.

The study will also investigate differences in unit costs of production caused by subgroups in the population of unskilled third class hires. Thus all inputs may have been constrained except unskilled third class with either previous job instability or no previous job experience. Even aside from the question of whether subsidies increased the employment of these undesirable persons, that amount of the subsidy allocated for desirable new workers could not have increased total employment and, with the absence of any correlation between subsidized training and promotion rates, did not increase wage benefits.

Obviously, it was impossible to observe the marginal physical products of laborers hired with differing general skills. In the previous section the available data was used to estimate expected productivity at any point in time relative to labor standards. Such estimates can be used if over the relevant range the expected production of the marginal welder hired as unskilled third class is the average production of all welders hired into that grade. This seems reasonable. In the classic example of diminishing returns to a factor, we consider the impact of an additional unit of labor on the output of a given piece of land. Thus we recognize the interdependence among a group of laborers. In the surveyed firm, one welder performing one task is largely independent of other welders performing similar tasks in other areas of the plant. This independence is subject to two restrictions. The first is a question of logistics, whether enough workers are available to deliver the required materials from warehouse to work areas, and the second, whether tasks are combined in some optimal mix. In other words, with the number of welders in the plant, we require a given output from pipefitters and sheetmetal workers to generate enough tasks to keep all the welders busy. Assuming that the firm has a production schedule and enough warehousemen, pipefitters, and sheetmetal workers to maintain it, we will use data that measures average as an estimate of marginal productivity.

Constraints on Unskilled Second Class Welders

In comparing unskilled second and third class hires, we are limited by available data on productivity to the analysis of one task in only one skill, welding. The surveyed task was both simpler than those assigned only to skilled welders and typical of tasks assigned to all recent unskilled hires. While the value of employees to the firm lies in their ability to perform a variety of tasks, observations on only one task should not seriously distort the results and should be sufficient to prove that welders hired as unskilled second class were a constrained input. The essential difference between unskilled second and third class welders was that the former had just enough ability to be placed directly into production while the latter were first placed in vestibule training. After vestibule training, unskilled third class hires were observed performing tasks similar to those assigned immediately to unskilled second class hires. This is the expected result if inputs of unskilled second class hires are constrained, because third class hires would perform at least some tasks that when possible would have been assigned to more skilled workers.

An estimate of the cost differential between unskilled second and third class hires will hinge on vestibule training costs. Certainly one cannot associate the costs of all vestibule training, applicable to a number of tasks, with the cost of the one surveyed task. Nevertheless, since the surveyed task is typical for an unskilled hire in the first six months of employment, it is consequently typical of the tasks for which he would be trained under the manpower program. But even if the unskilled second class hires performed more difficult tasks, we are concerned only with this hypothetical question: were unskilled second class hires a more efficient input for that precise mix of tasks usually assigned to unskilled third class hires?

To demonstrate that unskilled second class hires were a constrained input, all we need do is show that unskilled second class hires would be a less expensive labor input for the surveyed task. This is not difficult. First, unskilled second class hires have enough experience to do without the six weeks of vestibule training. Not only can they be placed immediately in production, but they must be at least as productive when hired as unskilled third class hires are after vestibule training. This must be true because the six weeks training is designed to bring a worker up to a minimum standard of general welding skill. Furthermore, unskilled second class hires can be expected to remain on board longer than unskilled third class hires. We can be confident of this because the coefficient on the variable for starting job classification was significant when length of service was regressed on the independent variables for the entire OJT and control group samples.

Let us compare two alternatives. The firm may hire either one person requiring vestibule training or it may hire one person with enough previous experience to go directly into production. Which alternative would offer a lower unit cost in the performance of those tasks typically assigned to unskilled third class hires? Assume for the moment that either one would remain as a stable long-term employee. The average cost of vestibule training is $715.80 per third class hire who completes the training.[3] But the unskilled second class hire earns higher wages. For example, he would start at $2.40 while unskilled third class starts vestibule training at $2.33. Knowing the mean length of time that workers spend in each wage classification as they are promoted up the wage ladder, we can calculate the wage savings from using an unskilled third class input. On average, unskilled second class hires reach the top of the wage ladder as skilled first class in twenty-seven months. Unskilled third class hires take thirty months. Thus, any wage savings disappear after thirty months. Over that interval, these savings total $345.

The cost of vestibule training is more than twice the wage saving when an unskilled second class hire is considered as an alternative. Moreover, the firm would benefit from more output by an unskilled second class hire because first he is in production for the six weeks that an unskilled third class is in vestibule training, and second he remains aboard on average for a longer time. Thus if we rephrase the question by asking what is the excess cost of using 100 unskilled third class hires to match the production expected from 100 unskilled second class hires, the excess costs must increase as a percentage of costs imposed by the unskilled second class. Since some unskilled third class hires will terminate during training, more than 100 unskilled third class persons must be hired to match the production of 100 unskilled second class hires.

The discussion does indicate that unskilled second class hires were a constrained resource. To subsidize a constrained input accomplishes nothing but a transfer of labor costs from the firm to taxpayers. Yet the firm received approximately $12.50 per week up to a maximum of twenty-six weeks for each subsidized unskilled second class hire. It also received $34 per week over six weeks in vestibule training and $12.50 per week over twenty weeks of formal on-the-job training of the subsidized unskilled third class welders. But both the marginal third and marginal second class hires were not subsidized. Thus, the marginal unskilled second class hire would be a less expensive input than the marginal third class hire. The manpower program must have subsidized a constrained input, which cannot increase the use of that input and only transfers income to the firm and its shareholders.

Constraints on Less Costly Unskilled Third Class Welders

The unskilled third class group was not homogeneous, and the hiring of many persons who either had no job experience or were short-term employees on their previous jobs did impose substantial excess costs on the firm. This can easily be demonstrated. The incidence of absenteeism was randomly distributed across the sample population. Productivity was dependent only on skills at time of hire and subsequent training. Only the distribution of length of service varied among definable subgroups of employees. We need two pieces of information: the observed frequency distribution on length of service for the entire sample population, and the observed distribution for persons with no previous job experience. With this information we can calculate the number with no previous job experience who would have to be hired as welders to match the output over 130 weeks of 100 persons who represent the actual mix of hires with previously stable, previously unstable, and no previous job experiences.

Because of the high turnover rate of those with no previous job experience, more than 100 of such persons must be hired. For example, with the actual mix of unskilled third class welders, 83 of the 100 would complete vestibule training and enter production. Substantially more than 100 persons with no previous experience would have to be hired if 83 were to remain to enter production. As an example of the program that was used to calculate the required feed-in of persons with no previous experience, beginning at time 0, when 83 were to remain to enter production, the number who would be needed in production at time $t=1$ is calculated by using

$$(3.2) \qquad \left[83 - f(0,t) \right] q(0,t)\,(.92) + \left[y_1 - f(1,t) \right] q(1,t)\,(.92) =$$
$$\left[83 - g(0,t) \right] q(0,t)\,(.92)$$

where

(a) y_1 is the required feed-in at time $t=1$;

(b) 83 equals the number who enter production at time t=0;

(c) $f(0,t)$ is the percentage of unskilled third class hires without previous experience who entered production at time 0 and were observed to terminate at time t;

(d) $f(1,t)$ is the percentage of unskilled third class hires without previous experience who enter production at time 1 and who can be expected to terminate by time t. If t=1, $f(1,1)$=0.

(e) .92 is the mean attendance rate for unskilled hires;

(f) $q(0,t)$ is productivity as the estimated ratio of actual hours to standard hours for unskilled aboard t weeks;

(g) $q(1,t)$ is the similar function for unskilled aboard $t-1$ weeks; and

(h) $g(0,t)$ is the percentage turnover for the actual mix of unskilled third class by time t.

One need only solve y_1 to determine the required feed-in at time 1 and calculate $y_1/.61$, where .61 is the observed percentage of such persons who complete vestibule training. This process can be repeated for t=2, including $\left[y_2 - f(2,t) \right]$ and substituting the known value for y_1 in (3.2).

Final calculations estimate that 225 unskilled third class welders with no previous job experience would have to be hired during the 130 weeks to match the production of 100 who reflect the actual mix of persons hired as unskilled third class. This number may seem excessive, but with the faster rate of turnover of unskilled without previous experience, more of these persons must be fed into the production process over time. Differences in turnover rates between those who are fed in and those who have remained from previous periods increase over time because the percentage of hires who terminate employment at any point in time is a monotonically decreasing function of length of service. Therefore, a small initial difference in turnover rates will cause a proportionately larger difference in the number who have to be hired if the two groups are to generate the same output. Using the $119.50 as the cost of vestibule training per man per week, the total cost of vestibule training for the 225 persons without previous job experience would be $190,000. This may be compared to a cost of $80,000 for the 100 persons from the actual mix of unskilled third class hires.

The data does suggest that using unskilled hires with a relatively high likelihood of short-term employment was an inefficient and expensive alternative to the firm as compared to using either unskilled second class, or for that matter, unskilled third class employees with a greater likelihood of remaining aboard for an extended period. The firm was aware of these excessive costs. Management continually complained of costs because of the unreliability of young people with little or no job experience. Yet at the same time, the firm was soliciting inexperienced high school students for employment after graduation. Not only was the firm unable to substitute cheaper alternatives, but it was soliciting applications from those known to be costly to hire and train. Such actions illustrate the constraints imposed upon the firm by the tightness of its local labor market.

Inflexibility of Relative Wages

With the existing wage rates, unskilled third class hires were more costly than both unskilled second class hires and definable subgroups among the unskilled third class. If the supply curves of labor had any slope to them at all, why did the shipbuilder not alter its relative wages, reducing its intake of more expensive labor and increasing its intake of less expensive?

The first point to emphasize is that in any adjustment of relative wages, its labor force would accept only movement of wages in one direction, upward. Thus for example, the firm could not lower the wages of the unskilled third class, but it might have been able to increase its wage to persons with sufficient previous experience to be classified as unskilled second class. Such action should draw more applicants who would not require vestibule training.

Although at existing wages, the cost differential between an unskilled second and third class hires may be three or four hundred dollars, a marginal change in the wage offered to applicants with previous welding experience may not be profitable. The point is that the supply curve of unskilled second class hires is not the relevant marginal outlay curve because the firm cannot merely increase its wage offer to job applicants who could be hired as unskilled second class. If it is to increase its offer to applicants, it must simultaneously increase the wages of unskilled second class already in its labor force. For example, if by increasing its wage offer from $2.40 to $2.45 it acquires one more applicant who would be hired as unskilled second class, its marginal outlay for that employee is not $2.45 but considerably more. By raising its price to $2.45 to get that applicant, it must also now pay $2.45 per hour to each of its unskilled second class employees. If it had 100 such persons in its labor force, the marginal outlay for the additional applicant would be $7.45 per hour and not $2.45. In effect, the firm is a monopsonist.[4] In facing an upward sloping supply curve its marginal outlay curve lies above its supply curve. As is well known, if this is so, the firm would maximize its profits by setting wages below those that would be determined in a competitive market. Therefore the marginal transformation conditions necessary for optimum economic efficiency would not be satisfied.

For the shipbuilder, raising its wage offer to attract persons experienced in the required skills may not have been consistent with profit maximization. Because this firm was exceptionally large, with over 5,000 employees, its marginal outlay curve may have been well above its supply curve. Substantiating this possibility, management was well aware of the cost of unskilled third class hires and continually complained of their inability to acquire more skilled labor at their current wages. Yet none of them thought of higher wages as a possible solution, and in fact said it could not afford higher wages.

Conclusions

All the data indicate that the shipbuilder's manpower programs did not benefit the subsidized trainees because it did not affect the marginal decisions of the firm. Admittedly, the sums of money involved were not large. A contract for hiring and training 200 welders cost $90,000 in public funds, $450 per employee. Although one could argue that the training program was not expensive, it was not worth much to trainees. This does not mean that employment with the firm was without value. After one year with the firm an unskilled third class hire was averaging $.48 more per hour than on his previous job. It was the subsidy that was worthless to the trainee because he could have earned that $.48 without it.

One may be tempted to argue that in so affluent a society $90,000 is not much to be concerned about. Two responses are appropriate. First, what was true of the shipbuilder's program may be true of other programs. Second, a subsidy of $90,000 may be socially undesirable while a considerably larger subsidy may in fact be desirable. This conclusion may be valid even if the larger subsidy does not affect marginal decisions as long as it does affect the total decision, that is, the existence or nonexistence of the firm. Simply by existing the shipbuilder is providing employment and training opportunities for persons considered in need of them. But $90,000 is not going to affect the total decision of a multimillion dollar operation. Once again the point is: if you do not pay much, chances are that you do not get much despite the benefit-cost ratio of approximately twenty which could be generated by considering $450 in costs against $.48 per hour over five years discounted at 10 percent.

Notes

1. Although the shipbuilder's personnel department faithfully interviewed each applicant, the interview did not appear to have a significant effect on the hiring decision. Personnel department employees admitted they were hiring anyone who could pass the physical examination and security check.

2. U.S., Manpower Administration, REQUEST FOR PROPOSAL MA-3 (Washington, D.C.: Government Printing Office, 1968).

3. All data on vestibule training costs and subsidy payments are from the cost and subsidy payments itemized in the firm's manpower contracts.

4. For another example of how monopsonistic behavior can affect resource allocation, see Paul W. MacAvoy, PRICE FORMATION IN NATURAL GAS FIELDS (New Haven: Yale University Press, 1962), 74-92. If the firm is monopsonistic, then this in itself could be a justification on efficiency grounds for a tax and transfer program. To be effective, such a program would have to affect the firm's marginal decisions, but the shipbuilder's manpower programs did not.

4 The Electronic Components Manufacturers

The analysis of the electronic components manufacturer will be structured like the study of the shipbuilder. First trainee and control groups will be compared to determine the effects of the subsidies on hiring decisions. Then the job performance of the two groups will be compared. Some of the calculations used to estimate costs and benefits will be unlike those performed for the shipbuilder's programs because the components manufacturer's program was vestibule rather than on the job. The programs of the two firms will be compared, but this is postponed until the next chapter, which concentrates on the policy recommendations that can be drawn from the study.

Comparison of Trainee and Control Groups

Table 4-1 gives mean values for the socioeconomic characteristics of a sample of people who received subsidized training and a control group trained by the firm's regular informal training procedure. The formal training was for a maximum of thirteen weeks of vestibule training during which the trainees were paid $2.00 per hour. After vestibule training, these people were transferred to

Table 4-1
Socioeconomic Characteristics

| | Women | | Men | |
| | OJT (N=40) | Control (N=20) | OJT (N=24) | Control (N=120) |
Variable				
Age	33.25	30.59	23.38	21.88
Percentage Non-White	80.00%	75.00%	45.83%	48.00%
Number of Dependents	2.12	1.70	1.13	.86
Percentage Raised and Educated in North	30.00%	15.00%	75.00%	52.38%
Labor Force Status	35.00%	40.00%	33.00%	43.00%
Number of Jobs Held Previous Year	1.33	1.45	1.63	1.52
Weeks Unemployed Previous Year	18.93*	9.80	9.63	6.76
Wage Previous Job	$2.00	$1.95	$2.29	$2.33
Number of Weeks on That Job	54.75	49.10	54.00	51.24
Starting Job Rate	2.60	2.50	3.90	3.85

*Significant at the .01 level

68

production, where they received informal training on the job. The members of the control group were placed immediately on the job, where they received informal training.

The control group was first structured to parallel the trainee group in the firm's broad definitions of families of jobs. In other words, if z percent of the trainees were assigned to jobs classified "mechanical assembler," then z percent of the control group was also classified under that label. It was then discovered that the control group had a larger percentage of men. More importantly, although men and women were hired under the same broad label, they were performing different jobs, that is assigned to different tasks. Therefore, both the control and trainee groups were restructured by distinguishing between men and women. Thus, for any group of women trained and hired as mechanical assemblers a parallel group representing a random sample of non-subsidized women hired as mechanical assemblers was also selected to maintain the same proportion of female mechanical assemblers in both groups. Table 4-1 lists a control group for both sexes, where the control group for either sex parallels the trainee group in broad job classifications.

The table indicates that the trainee and control groups are very similar in socioeconomic characteristics. The only statistically significant differences occurred in the region of the country in which persons were raised and educated and the extent of previous unemployment among the women. But this statistically significant difference was caused by three women in the subsidized group who had been unemployed for more than 99 weeks, obviously not seeking work.

Even if we were prepared to argue that the firm had a relative preference for hiring persons raised and educated somewhere other than the North, or that it avoided women who had been out of the job market for an extended period, still it would seem that most persons hired under the subsidy program would have been eligible for employment without subsidized training. For example, 30 percent of the female trainees were raised and educated in the North, as compared to 15 percent of the female control group. The difference in the composition of the trainee group, which is the 15 percent differential between the percentage of the trainee and control groups raised and educated in the North, is only six women of the forty who received subsidized training. We may add to this number the two women who were unemployed at least 99 weeks and were *not* raised and educated in the North. Thus the composition of the trainee group differed from the control group in only eight of forty women or 20 percent. As for men, the differential between 75 percent of the trainees raised and educated in the North and approximately 50 percent for the control group translates into six of twenty-four or 25 percent of the trainee population.

Even if the firm had aversions to northerners and to those women previously unemployed for an extended period, most of the subsidized men and women would have been eligible for employment without the subsidies. Besides aversions based on these two socioeconomic characteristics would seem irrational especially in a tight labor market because subsequent data will reveal that they had no significant effect on job performance measures. Therefore it would be more logical to argue that all persons hired under the subsidy program would not otherwise have been disqualified for employment because of factors such as age, education, previous employment, or northern raised and educated. Furthermore, the firm was not getting any applicants with previous experience in the surveyed skills. This suggests that persons who received subsidies would not have been disqualified for employment because they lacked previous experience in the required skills. Thus we can conclude that the subsidy program had little or no impact in increasing the employment of persons eligible for subsidies.

The Multivariate Analysis

Once again, we are concerned with assessing the independent impact of subsidized training upon job performance as measured by turnover, absenteeism, and productivity. Separate regressions will be performed for men and women. This standardizes for sex. With little or no substitution of men for women across jobs, any observations that these cost parameters differed between men and women are irrelevant in comparing the costs of hiring various groups of employees. Ordinary least squares will be used because the multicollinearity does not appear to be nearly as serious as for the shipbuilder. As Table 4-2 indicates,

Table 4-2
F **Tests on Each Independent Variable**

Variable	All Men (N=45)	All Women (N=61)
Age	2.971	2.344
Race	2.189	1.881
Number of Dependents	2.561	1.819
Years of Education	3.537	1.658
Region Raised and Educated	4.278	.923
Labor Force Status	1.573	3.149
Number of Jobs in the Year Preceding Employment with the Firm	89.432	60.159
Weeks Unemployed During that Year	97.034	56.627
Weeks on Last Job	4.632	5.412
Subsidized Training	2.677	2.272
Determinant of the Correlation Matrix	.003	.005

the only variables that appear to be strongly colinear are those that measure the number of previous jobs and the extent of previous unemployment. Therefore, subject to the restriction that the independent impacts of these two variables cannot be assessed and the *t* test may be unreasonably small, ordinary least squares is an acceptable estimation technique.

Turnover

The dependent variable was length of service with the firm. This variable covered a maximum of twenty-six weeks on the job for the control group. For the trainee group, it measured the sum up to twenty-six weeks of time in vestibule training plus time on the job. We could have measured only time on the job for the trainees, but this would not have yielded usable information. If only time on the job were regressed on the independent variables, we could expect vestibule training to have a significant impact even if the distribution of length of service from the beginning of training was not affected by it. If most turnover is by short-term employees, these people may weed themselves out during vestibule training, while the employees who progress to production are usually long term. Thus we could observe a significant impact for vestibule training without gaining any information about an essential question. Did the resources associated with subsidized vestibule training, not only the skill training but also the counseling and supportive services, have any real impact on extending the employment of subsidized persons?

Using total time in training and on the job also provides information about another important question. Even if vestibule training did not alter the distribution of length of service, vestibule training by weeding out short-term employees must reduce the turnover of those placed on the job. This result, combined with the observed distribution of length of service, provides necessary information to assess the costs and benefits of subsidized training.

Table 4-3 gives the coefficient and *t* tests of two regressions, one each for men and women, on the independent variables listed in the table. As with the shipbuilder, labor force status prior to employment with the firm had a statistically significant impact. More important, subsidized vestibule training, coded as a 1,0 dummy, was not statistically significant.

Table 4-4 gives the mean values of the sum of time in training and on the job for the trainee and control groups. It also gives the percentages retained from the two groups after twenty-six weeks. These numbers can be compared to those which are the percentage of persons retained thirteen weeks after they were placed on the job and their mean weeks on the job. The data in the table reveals that vestibule training may have weeded out short-term employees.

Table 4-3
Coefficients of Regression with Length on Service as Dependent Variable

Variable	Men	Women
Age	.2135	.1963
	(.1762)	(.0739)
Race	.9876	1.1432
	(.4371)	(1.1306)
Number of Dependents	1.1310	2.6410
	(.4132)	(.5734)
Raised and Educated in the North	.1176	−1.473
	(1.132)	(−1.4338)
Labor Force Status	2.4310**	3.7410***
	(2.6410)	(3.1475)
Number of Jobs in Year Preceding Employment with the Firm	−1.3781	−.8431
	(−1.1320)	(−1.4220)
Weeks Unemployed During that Year	−2.0318	−.9462
	(−1.6211)	(−.0419)
Weeks on Last Job	.2147*	.3401*
	(1.9431)	(1.8320)
Subsidized Training	−1.3120	−.9125
	(−.7615)	(−1.0310)
R^2	.1431	.1221
F	4.132	5.1364
Intercept	11.8261	5.0963

*Significant at .10 level
**Significant at .02 level
***Significant at .01 level

Table 4-4
Retention Rates and Mean Length of Service

	Women		Men	
Variables	Control	Trainees	Control	Trainees
Percentage Who Remained 26 Weeks	80.0%	75.6%	67.0%	67.0%
Mean Weeks	22.5	19.27	17.33	17.00
Percentage Who Remained 13 Weeks on the Job	85.0%	91.2%	76.2%	88.9%
Mean Weeks on the Job	11.55	12.32	11.09	12.22

Absenteeism

Absenteeism was measured as the ratio of hours in attendance to the sum of hours in attendance, plus hours tardy, plus the number of days absent times eight hours. As with the shipbuilder, none of the surveyed socioeconomic characteristics had a statistically significant impact on the incidence of absenteeism. All variables, including vestibule training, were highly insignificant for both men and women, and F tests on the impact of all variables taken together were less than one. We can only conclude that absenteeism was randomly distributed among the sample population and that vestibule training did not reduce it.

Productivity

Productivity was measured as the ratio of hours required to produce a given amount to standard hours budgeted. Two tasks were surveyed, one each for men and women. Thus, we are using one task for each in comparing the productivity of male and female trainees against male and female control groups.

The regression model is specified to be

$$(4.1) \qquad P_t = \alpha(t)^{\beta_1}(xt)^{\beta_2}(x)^{\beta_3}.$$

Thus (xt) tests for differences in the curvature of the learning curve and x tests for differences in the intercept. We do expect β_3 to be statistically significant and negative, not merely because supervisors have stated that trainees tend to be more productive when hired, but simply because vestibule training should have some impact. Also we expect β_2 to be statistically significant and positive, because line supervisors reported that the superior productivity of trainees lasted only about a month, after which non-subsidized employees caught up.

Table 4-5 gives the t values for the independent variables. Once again to protect the interests of the firm, the regression coefficients are not given. For both regressions, the intercept term (α) was statistically significant and positive,

Table 4-5
t Tests and R^2's for Productivity Regressions

Variables	Men	Women
Intercept	4.731	3.872
β_1	−2.506	−3.154
β_2	1.876	1.634
β_3	−1.472	−2.105
R^2	.3142	.3921

and β_1 was statistically significant and negative. Moreover, the signs of β_2 and β_3 were as expected in both regressions. Among these, however, the only very statistically significant coefficient was β_3 in the regression for women. This coefficient was significant at the .05 level. Nevertheless, if we do construct the learning curve for the control group as

$$(4.2) \qquad P_t = \alpha(t)^{\beta_1},$$

and for the sample of trainees as

$$(4.3) \qquad P_s = \alpha(t)^{(\beta_1 + \beta_2)} e^{\beta_3}$$

the point of intercept between the two curves is at approximately four weeks for men and seven weeks for women. The integral of (4.3) was subtracted from the integral of (4.2) for both men and women. For example integrals for the estimated functions (4.3) and (4.2) for men were taken from zero to four weeks. This difference was then multiplied by 40 to calculate the difference in hour inputs required to perform four weeks of a standardized task. As a check on the validity of these results, the difference in the values of the integrals was calculated from four to 100 weeks and multiplied by 40. If male trainees caught up in four weeks with no differences in productivity afterwards, and if our estimated functions are to be acceptable, the differences in the values of the integrals from four to an arbitrary 100 weeks for men and seven to 100 weeks for women should be so small as to be insignificant. This was true.

Thus if we accept the estimates of β_2 and β_3 we can conclude that the estimate functions do indicate small productivity gains, approximately thirty-five hours of work for women and twenty-two for men. These gains are small because the differences in productivity disappeared in less than two months. This is not surprising. Line supervisors wished to have subsidized trainees assigned to them because they were more productive initially and therefore required less supervision. But supervision was an input into informal training. Since subsidized trainees were relatively more productive when placed on the job, supervisors believed that it could reduce the informal on-the-job training for them. In effect, subsidized vestibule training was a substitute for informal on-the-job training.

The observation that line supervisors like subsidized vestibule training because it allowed them to reduce time devoted to training indicates that the supervisors received benefits from the subsidies. Some of the benefits of the subsidies might have been absorbed in slack as free time for supervisors. Of course supervisors may have devoted this time to some other productive activity within the firm. If they did, benefits from the substitution of formal for informal training would in part accrue to the firm and its shareholders.

Program Benefits

Benefits for the Firm

The one and only cost parameter not favorably affected by subsidized vestibule training was absenteeism. Persons who completed such training and were placed on a job were no less likely to be absent than the control group. On the other hand, turnover was reduced by vestibule training. This reduction did not occur because vestibule training induced workers to lengthen their term of service, measured as the sum of weeks in training and weeks on the job. Vestibule training weeded out short-term employees before they were placed on the job. This is important because the firm does invest in the informal training of its employees after they are placed on the job. Weeding out short-term employees would generate a larger return per informal training dollar. Subsidized vestibule training also increased productivity, at least over the initial weeks on the job, and substituted for informal training, yielding a cost saving.

Although the firm did receive benefits from formal vestibule training, the program was probably not an efficient investment. The firm estimated vestibule training costs to be $25 per day per employee. This includes $16 in wages, with the balance for materials, supplies, training instructors, and administrative overhead. No opportunity cost was included on the plant floor space turned over to training, because the firm used excess plant capacity. We can estimate costs by multiplying $25 by 65 days for those who completed vestibule training. For example, the cost for the thirty-three women who completed it would be $53,625. We must add to this the cost of the eight women who terminated while in training. To do this, we make some simplifying assumptions which will overestimate the costs of their training. The $25 per day included an average cost of administrative and training services. These costs are indivisible. If a woman terminates, the firm is still burdened with approximately $9.00 per day of such costs. Actually, the cost is less than $9.00 because the use of training materials and supplies would be reduced. Nevertheless, let us assume that the firm established its program under the assumption that the forty-one women who began training would complete it. When a woman terminates, the firm cannot reduce its administrative and training instructor costs. Thus the cost of these eight women would be $25 per each day that they were aboard and $9.00 thereafter. These costs are $6,510, making total costs of training $60,135.

It is extremely doubtful that the small increase in productivity, the weeding out of some short-term employees, and the reduction in informal training provided benefits that would have been sufficient to induce the firm to spend so much of its own money. If the benefits of improved job performance accrued to the firm and if the vestibule program had proved efficient, one would expect it to have considered initiating such training at its own expense. But the firm was without vestibule training before subsidies, used this training only for subsidized employees, and has no plan for such a program after its subsidies are phased out.

The vestibule training program was probably inefficient. On the other hand, with the subsidy payments it was also profitable. Although the firm spent $25 per day for vestibule training of one employee over thirteen weeks, it received as compensation $11.50 per day up to fifty-two weeks.[1] Thus the firm received $2,900 for each trainee who remained aboard for one year, while the vestibule training of that person cost only $1,625. The difference between $2,990 and $1,625 is presumably for training on the job. But since the trainee would have been eligible for employment without subsidies, $1,360 of the subsidy is payment for costs that the firm would have incurred with or without subsidies. The $1,360 represents a transfer between taxpayers and stockholders.

We have observations over twenty-six weeks from the beginning of vestibule training. With this information, we can calculate the total subsidy payments up to twenty-six weeks for the hiring of the forty-one women. This payment totals $49,047.50. The firm also received $65.50 per each additional day that the thirty-one women remain, aboard or in other words, $1,782.50 per week. At this rate, the firm would be more than compensated for its vestibule training costs if the thirty-one women remained aboard an additional 6.5 weeks. Since most turnover occurs shortly after persons are hired (eight of the ten women trainees who terminated did so within twelve weeks), one can be confident that the firm will receive a total subsidy payment substantially in excess of its total vestibule training costs. The firm is therefore making windfall profits on its subsidy payments alone without even considering its other benefits from vestibule training.

One could make similar calculations and reach similar conclusions about the vestibule training of men. The firm receives compensation for both vestibule and on-the-job training costs. But only the vestibule training imposes costs that the firm would not willingly have assumed in the employment and training of persons who would be eligible for employment without subsidized vestibule training. The result of the program is a perverse distribution of program benefits caused by two factors. First, the firm and its shareholders are oversubsidized for initiating the manpower programs because the subsidy payments exceed the true cost of such programs to the firm. Second, the benefits generated by the implementation of such a program, namely the reduced turnover and increased productivity of persons placed on the job, accrue to the firm and not to the employees.

Benefits for Employees

The trainees did not receive benefits in the form of higher wages than non-trainees. The vestibule training did not affect either entry port jobs and starting wages or the rate of promotion of subsidized as compared to non-subsidized employees. The subsidized could have been hired into the same entry port jobs for the same wages without subsidies. Once hired, they could be promoted through the system of posted job openings. Interested employees would apply, and the firm would eliminate unqualified applicants. Identifying those who can adequately do a set of tasks somewhat different from those they previously performed, the firm promoted the worker with the most seniority. Since the control and trainee group were identical in socioeconomic characteristics, and since productivity differences between the two groups lasted for only a few weeks, one would not expect any significant differences in the average number of promotions in the groups. There were none. Trainee men placed on a job received two, trainee women zero promotions. Control group men received two and women one. No trainee women and only one in twenty control group women were promoted to a higher wage job, one in nine trainee men and slightly less than one in ten control men received similar promotions. We can conclude that vestibule training did not increase hourly earnings. Such training neither increased starting wages nor promotions for the trainee group as opposed to the control group.

Vestibule training did, however, generate some benefits for trainees. In establishing vestibule training, the firm attempted to estimate its need at that time when trainees would be completing training. Actually the firm may have underestimated somewhat. This is indicated first by the fact that we were able to isolate a control group hired without subsidies in the period when trainees were being placed on the job. Second, trainees who were placed on the job did not remain in vestibule training for the full thirteen weeks. They averaged only ten weeks of such training. The firm appears to have been willing to transfer such persons after a reasonable period of vestibule training to a job as soon as a vacancy was available.

If vestibule training resulted in the employment of persons ten weeks before job vacancies were available, this must create some income benefits to subsidized employees. However, the maximum benefit to workers with socioeconomic characteristics typical of the trainees would be $800. The maximum could be realized under either one of two conditions. First, without the option of vestibule training, the trainee may have been unemployed over the full ten weeks. This seems unlikely. The other condition seems more likely. The trainee might have been able to find a job as an alternative to training, but in doing so, he would displace the employment of another person, who in his turn would displace the employment of someone else. This process could continue, eventually generating a total of approximately ten weeks of unemployment among workers with socioeconomic characteristics typical of the subsidized employees. Thus if the subsidized program creates ten weeks of training at $2.00 per hour, $800 in benefits may have been generated by the program. But the point to emphasize is that no more than $800 would be created. The program created only a ten-week employment opportunity. After that, the job opportunity could have existed with or without subsidies.

Summary

A critical assessment of this firm's manpower program must hinge on this observation: the firm would receive $2,990 for the training of one person, while that training generated no more than $800 in income benefits for the disadvantaged. In the meantime, the firm has received benefits from subsidy payments in excess of costs as well as from some increase in productivity. Offsetting the increase in productivity, however, is the efficiency costs imposed by the program. The small increases in productivity and the weeding out of short-term employees did not appear to have increased returns enough to cover the costs of the investment in human capital. This inefficiency may be tolerable in the interests of equity, but the program generated no more than $800 in benefits for each person who completed the program. The remainder of the benefits accrued to the firm and its shareholders, persons who are on the average wealthier than the average taxpayer. With this perverse distribution of benefits we may have some serious doubts whether this program should have been funded. Certainly it has not had the unambiguously desirable impact that some cost-benefit studies have credited to manpower programs.

Note

1. All data on costs and subsidy payments are taken from the firm's manpower program contract.

5

Conclusions and Policy Recommendations

Comparison of the Two Empirical Studies

In the shipbuilder and in the electronic components manufacturer, the sample of subsidized trainees could not be statistically distinguished from the samples of workers who were not subsidized. This is strong evidence that the training programs did not affect hiring decisions. They did not reduce the incidence of unemployment or low wage jobs within the target population qualifying for aid under manpower programs.

Both firms faced similar external labor market conditions when they implemented subsidized training. The shipbuilder was rapidly expanding against an inadequate supply of laborers with previous experience in the required skills. It bore considerable costs in training young, inexperienced hires. Subsidized training minimized that burden. Thus subsidized on-the-job and vestibule training substituted for the training which non-subsidized employees received and provided windfall gains to the shipbuilder. A general tightness of the labor market also forced the electronic components manufacturer to use labor that it felt was undesirable even for the relatively low wage jobs in his plant. The laborers used for such jobs were younger, blacker, and less well educated than they were when the labor market was not as tight. As with the shipbuilder, a tight labor market had eroded hiring criteria until normal hires for specified jobs had the socioeconomic characteristics required for manpower subsidies. When they were not required to lower hiring standards, both firms contracted for manpower programs. Because standards were not lowered, the programs provided few if any benefits for the disadvantaged.

Although the effects of both firms' programs were similar, they were not identical. Unlike the shipbuilder, where the trainees received no identifiable increments to earnings for trainees, the component manufacturer's program did generate some incremental earnings for trainees. Its vestibule training gave ten-weeks' wages before job vacancy occurred within the plant. Thus it did create limited additional income for the disadvantaged. Of course, the electronic component manufacturer's program was far more expensive than any of the shipbuilder's program. The most costly of the shipbuilder's programs budgeted $450 per trainee but the electronic component manufacturer's budgeted almost $3,000. One must question the social value of a program that imposes a cost of $3,000 on taxpayers in exchange for $800 in benefits created per training slot.

None of the surveyed programs had any measurable effect on promotions.

79

This is not surprising. The program of both firms had no statistically significant impact on job performance indicators such as absenteeism and turnover. Although the electronic components manufacturer's program did increase productivity somewhat during initial employment, this increase disappeared well before trainees were eligible for promotion. Besides eligibility criteria are poorly related to job performance. Seniority and not exceptional job performance was the principal consideration in promotion decisions.

Although trainees received no measurable gains from the shipbuilder's programs and only minor gains from the component manufacturer's, both firms benefited from their manpower contracts. But these benefits did not result because the programs increased efficiency. The shipbuilder's programs were probably no more or less efficient than the programs that would have been instituted if subsidies were not available, and the electronic components manufacturer's training procedures appear to have been relatively inefficient under its subsidy program. The shipbuilder was able to transfer to the government training costs it would have incurred without subsidies. The electronic component manufacturer received some slight productivity increases and subsidy payments greatly in excess of vestibule costs.

Limitations on the Analysis

The conclusion that two manpower programs—and probably others—have resulted in an inequitable redistribution from taxpayers to shareholders with minimal benefits to trainees was based on empirical study and theory both short run and static. The short-run and static analysis is not disturbing because hiring is a short-run decision. However, the analysis was limited to only the distribution of direct outputs. The static analysis was not suitable for assessing indirect program benefits such as the income generated by a firm's reinvestment of its share of program direct benefits. If the subsidy programs increased aggregate demand by increasing investment demand, some benefits may have trickled down to those low income people who were first intended to receive the benefits of the manpower programs.

Even if the manpower programs expanded aggregate demand, this does not exempt the programs from criticism for their perverse redistribution of direct program benefits. If the benefits to low income workers of manpower programs come mostly from the expansion of aggregate demand, which causes employers to hire farther down the queue, it would seem that a simple across-the-board reduction in taxes would be preferable. This reduction could be structured to bring about an equivalent increase in aggregate demand without the initial perverse distribution.

Policy Alternatives

Reform for Manpower Programs

The fundamental problem with selection of manpower programs has been inadequate information. Administrators of these programs have not known enough about the hiring, training, and promotion activities that firms would undertake without subsidy programs, nor have they known the job performance of subsidized compared to non-subsidized workers. Both are crucial in selecting firms to be subsidized and in determining the appropriate subsidy. Clearly, a change in the procedures for designing and letting manpower contracts would be desirable.

Manpower program administrators should be aware that a firm requesting contracts may be receptive to hiring the disadvantaged because labor market conditions have reduced hiring criteria.[1] A firm seeking on-the-job training contracts or regularly hiring the graduates of institutional programs should be investigated, when possible, to determine its normal non-subsidized source of hires for those same jobs assigned to the subsidized. Such an investigation would not take much time for either the manpower program administrator or for the firm. It requires merely a survey of records in the personnel department of any firm. To determine whether non-subsidized hires would be similar or dissimilar in socioeconomic characteristics to subsidized hires is not time consuming or expensive.

Although administrators may easily identify firms that would substantially reduce hiring criteria if granted a subsidy, such information is not in itself sufficient to determine the appropriate amount of the subsidy. The excess costs imposed on a firm willing to lower hiring criteria need not equal formal training costs of manpower programs because of differences in other aspects of job performance. If the firms were willing to alter hiring or promotion criteria substantially, it would be impossible to predict before employment the job performance of its subsidized persons. Even ex-post estimates, like those performed in this book, are extremely time consuming and expensive. They can be done only for firms that either have been keeping or are prepared to initiate extremely detailed records on the performance of each sampled employee. Few firms may be both willing and able to cooperate in such a study. Furthermore, the time, money, and talents currently available to manpower program administrators would be inadequate to undertake such studies. Thus subsidy levels probably will continue to be determined without sufficient information.

If the subsidy for either on-the-job or institutional training is determined without detailed cost information, then any upper limit on the subsidy per trainee is arbitrary. A successful manpower program should deal only with firms that would not hire or promote persons eligible for a subsidy without it. But the study of two firms in this book suggests that with subsidies of $3,000 or less per hire current manpower programs may not be attractive to firms that would have to substantially alter hiring policy. The obvious solution is to raise subsidy payments and exclude those firms that would be the principal beneficiaries instead of their trainees. But if current subsidy levels have not always generated benefits in excess costs, then one must wonder whether increasing the costs of manpower programs would bring incremental benefits sufficient to more than offset incremental costs. In other words, increasing subsidies is the obvious method for increasing benefits to trainees, but whether more expensive programs would be socially desirable is another question that current information cannot answer.

Expansion of Aggregate Demand

If subsidies are one technique for altering hiring and promotion criteria and creating income benefits for the disadvantaged, tightening the labor market by an expansion of aggregate demand is another. As the labor market tightens more and more firms will shift without subsidies to laborers eligible for subsidies. These firms should no longer be granted subsidies. Experiences during World War II in the successful training of laborers to perform very sophisticated jobs indicates that this shift will occur.[2] We could improve the training and employment of our urban poor and other low wage earners, if we are prepared to progressively tighten the labor market through macroeconomic policies. For example, both surveyed firms complained of shortages among the laborers they would prefer to hire.

Of course our willingness to engage in expansionary macroeconomic policies is limited by inflation. But given the poor performance of many existing manpower programs, and given the perverse redistribution of income and consumption these programs can and do cause, perhaps the best we could do would be to eliminate the least desirable of them and concentrate on expansionary macroeconomic policies, accepting as much inflation as politically tolerable. This would generate, it might be hoped, the training and employment opportunities that have not come under many federally subsidized manpower programs. It may be that a prolonged tight labor market, giving low income people new job opportunities, training, and seniority rights, is the beginning of the answer. Combined with improved educational facilities in our urban centers, an increased willingness of colleges and universities to lower entrance standards to accept minorities, and vigorous efforts by civil rights organizations, a simple expansion of aggregate demand may begin to solve the problems that some manpower programs have barely touched. If these developments occur, little justification remains to invest in at least that subgroup of manpower programs that may create few new job opportunities, effect perverse redistributions, and displace other federal activities which on average do generate equity benefits.

Notes

1. Dissatisfaction with manpower programs appears to be spreading. See for example, U.S., Senate, Committee on Labor and Public Welfare, MANPOWER DEVELOPMENT AND TRAINING LEGISLATION, 1970, hearings before the subcommittee on Employment, Manpower, and Poverty, Senate, on S.3867, S.2838, S.3878, 91st Cong., 1st and 2d sess. 1970. Note especially that Greenberg (Part 4, 2350) and Bechel (Part 4, 2376-2378) assert that at least some manpower programs have benefited mostly firms. These statements should be read with Arnold R. Weber (Part 4, 2445) who defends the Labor Department's policies for awarding manpower contracts. It is also interesting to note that as unemployment increased, the MANPOWER REPORT OF THE PRESIDENT, 1971 (48) states that "few opportunities were open to the hard-core unemployed in on-the-job training," and $49 million was transferred out of the JOBS program.

2. For example, Ray Marshall, THE NEGRO WORKER (New York: Random House, 1967), 96, Table 6:2 indicates that the percentage of blacks among craftsmen, foremen, and kindred workers increased by .9 percent between 1940-1944. This can be compared to a .8 percent increase between 1944 and 1962.

Appendixes

Appendix: Principal Components in Regression Analysis

Multicollinearity presents two problems. First, given strong colinearity between any two variables, we cannot isolate the independent impact of either simply because they move together. Second the values of t tests on colinear variables may be unreasonable. Thus if any two independent variables, i and j, are correlated, then a_{ii} and a_{jj}, diagonal elements of $(X'X)^{-1}$, where X is the data matrix, should be quite large, reducing the t value and suggesting statistical insignificance. On the other hand, if some other variable, k, is uncorrelated with i or j, then one would expect a reasonable value for a_{kk} and therefore a reasonable t value on that variable.

One technique for assuring that the data matrix is not nearly singular, which is the cause of the exploded values for the diagonal elements of the inverse, is principal component analysis. Given the generalized regression formal

(A.1) $\qquad Y = Gd + \mu,$

where G represents a matrix of m observations on n variables and d is a column vector of n coefficients, one normally wishes to estimate $y = dg$. Unfortunately, a subset of $(n-r)$ variables including those such as years in the labor force and weeks previous job held are interdependent. The remaining r variables are independent of each other and of the set $(n-r)$. Consequently, Gd can be considered as $Xa+Zb$ with the matrices X and Z having dimensions of $(n-r)\ m$ and $(r\times m)$ respectively, and the dimensions of a and b being $(n-1) \times 1$ and $(r\times 1)$. The objective of principal components is to isolate the independent dimensions among the $(n-r)$ variables composing the X matrix.

After the set of variables composing X are identified, principal component analysis constructs new variables which are linear combinations of X. In other words, a matrix V of $(n-r)\ xm$ dimensions is selected such that $(VC)a=Xa$, but as distinct from $|X'X|$, $|V'V|$ is not nearly zero. In fact, $V'V$ is an orthogonal matrix. The dimension of C is $(n-r) \times (n-r)$. The first component, $(V_{1j})(C_{j1})$, $j=1$, $(n-r)$, explains the maximum amount of variation in the original explanatory variables and is independent of all other components. This procedure is duplicated in calculating the second component. Simply stated, the observed information on $(n-r)$ variables is redefined relative to a new set of axes as determined by V. In other words, a linear combination of explanatory variables is constructed as a new variable, a principal component, which is independent of every other component. Presumably, this allows an evaluation of the independent dimensions among a colinear set. For example, if two variables such as years of education and region of the country in which a person was raised and educated, either North and South, are highly correlated with a component, we may conclude that this component reflects the quantity and quality of formal education.

Such an approach has drawbacks. First, since the component variables are redefined linear combinations of a set of variables, one can no longer place objective labels on them. Such a variable cannot, for example, be simply defined as years of education. One can attempt to identify a component by correlating the original explanatory variables with the components, but ultimately such a process leads to a subjective interpretation of the meaning and consequently to a subjective interpretation of the impact of any of the original explanatory variables. Second elasticity estimates on the components are meaningless. Percentage changes in the dependent variables cannot be related to a percentage change in any original variable. Third, principal component analysis is equivalent to the introduction of constraints in ordinary least squares. This procedure consequently imposes a cost because unlike ordinary least squares, it does not produce unbiased estimates. For example, given ($n - r$) colinear variables, ($n - r$) components can be constructed where the first component explains the maximum amount of variation in the original explanatory variables. The second component explains the maximum amount of the remaining variation. Continuing this procedure, one typically finds that the last few components $s, s+1, \ldots, (n-r)$ explain very little of the variation. These components are generally dropped from further analysis. Although this procedure does reduce the degrees of freedom that one must consider, by dropping the last components, we introduce ($n-r-s+1$) constraints into ordinary least squares. Unconstrained ordinary least squares generate unbiased estimates. On the other hand, performing an ordinary least squares regression on ($s-1$) components represents a constrained minimization problem where the estimated coefficients can no longer be proved to be unbiased.

Principal component analysis does, however, have some value for the type of analysis performed in this book. Given strong multicollinearity between variables such as age and years in the labor force, we cannot isolate the independent impact of these two variables. Thus the fact that one can neither place objective labels on the components nor make elasticity estimates given the estimated coefficients on those components does not impose particularly burdensome costs. On the other hand, the principal components analysis will be helpful because we are concerned with performing a reasonably reliable statistical test to indicate at least whether any set of variables acting together had a significant impact. Ordinary least squares may indicate statistical insignificance, but we cannot place much confidence on such tests. If on the other hand, we could identify a principal component that reflects primarily the impact of age and years in the labor force, and if a t test indicates that the coefficient on that component is statistically insignificant from zero, then we can more confidently eliminate that component from consideration when explaining the incidence of turnover or absenteeism.

References

Reference

Anderson, W.H.L. "Trickling Down: The Relationship Between Economic Growth and the Extent of Poverty Among American Families." QUARTERLY JOURNAL OF ECONOMICS, 78 (Nov. 1964), 511-524.

Arrow, Kenneth J. and Alain C. Enthoven. "Quasi-Concave Programming." ECONOMETRICA, 29 (Oct. 1961), 779-800.

Becker, Gary S. HUMAN CAPITAL: A THEORETICAL AND EMPIRICAL ANALYSIS WITH SPECIAL REFERENCE TO EDUCATION. New York: Columbia University Press, 1964.

Bishop, G.A. "The Tax Burden by Income Class." NATIONAL TAX JOURNAL, 14 (Mar. 1961), 41-59.

Borus, Micheal E. "A Benefit-Cost Analysis of Retraining the Unemployed." YALE ECONOMIC REVIEW, 6 (Fall, 1964), 371-429.

Borus, Micheal E., John Brennan, and Sidney Rosen. "A Benefit-Cost Analysis of the Neighborhood Youth Corps: The Out-of-Plant Program in Indiana." JOURNAL OF HUMAN RESOURCES, 5 (Spring, 1970), 139-159.

Doeringer, Peter B. and Micheal J. Piore. INTERNAL LABOR MARKETS AND MANPOWER ANALYSIS. Lexington, Mass.: Heath Lexington Books, 1971.

Doeringer, Peter B. and Micheal J. Piore. "Labor Market Adjustments." INDUSTRIAL RELATIONS RESEARCH ASSOCIATION: PROCEEDINGS.

Gillespie, W. Irwin. "Effect of Public Expenditures on the Distribution of Income." ESSAYS IN FISCAL FEDERALISM. Edited by Richard A. Musgrave. Washington, D.C.: The Brookings Institute, 1965.

Hochman, Harold M. and James D. Rodgers. "Pareto Optimal Redistribution." AMERICAN ECONOMIC REVIEW, 59 (Sept. 1969), 542-557.

Kerr, Clark. "The Balkanization of Labor Markets." LABOR MOBILITY AND ECONOMIC OPPORTUNITY. Edited by E. Wright Bakke. Cambridge, Mass.: MIT Press, 1954.

Lester, Richard A. HIRING PRACTICES AND LABOR COMPETITION. Princeton, New Jersey: Princeton University Press, 1954.

Levitan, Sar A. "Manpower Aspects of the Economic Opportunity Act." INDUSTRIAL RELATIONS RESEARCH ASSOCIATION, 21 (1968), 172-181.

MacAvoy, Paul E. PRICE FORMATION IN NATURAL GAS FIELDS. New Haven, Conn.: Yale University Press, 1962.

Main, Earl D. "A Nationwide Evaluation of MDTA Institutional Job Training." THE JOURNAL OF HUMAN RESOURCES, 3 (May, 1968), 159-170.

Mangum, Garth. "Evaluating Federal Manpower Programs." INDUSTRIAL RELATIONS RESEARCH ASSOCIATION, 21 (1968), 161-171.

Marshall, Ray. THE NEGRO WORKER. New York: Random House, 1967.

Musgrave, Richard A. et. al. "Distribution of Tax Payments by Income Groups:

A Case Study for 1948 " NATIONAL TAX JOURNAL, 4 (Mar. 1951), 1-53.

New York Stock Exchange. Board of Governors. FACT BOOK. New York: New York Stock Exchange, 1970.

Oi, Walter. "Labor as a Quasi-fixed Factor." THE JOURNAL OF POLITICAL ECONOMY, 70 (Dec. 1962), 538-555.

Page, David A. "Retraining Under the Manpower Development Act: A Cost-Benefit Analysis." PUBLIC POLICY, 13 (1964).

Piore, Micheal J. "Impact of Labor Markets on the Design and Selection of Productive Technique within the Manufacturing Plant." QUARTERLY JOURNAL OF ECONOMICS, 62 (Nov. 1968), 602-620.

Pechman, Joseph A. FEDERAL TAX POLICY. Washington, D.C.: The Brookings Institute, 1966.

Reynolds, Lloyd. THE STRUCTURE OF LABOR MARKETS. New York: Harper & Brothers, 1959.

Ribich, Thomas I. EDUCATION AND POVERTY. Washington, D.C.: The Brookings Institute, 1968.

Somers, Gerald. "Retraining, an Evaluation of Gains and Costs." EMPLOYMENT POLICY AND THE LABOR MARKET. Edited by A.M. Ross. Berkeley: The University California Press, 1965.

Somers, Gerald and Ernst Stromsdorfer. "A Benefit-Cost Analysis of Manpower Retraining," INDUSTRIAL RELATIONS RESEARCH ASSOCIATION, 17 (1964), 172-194.

Thurow, Lester C. "The Changing Structure of Unemployment: An Economic Study." REVIEW OF ECONOMICS AND STATISTICS, 47 (May, 1965), 137-149.

Turner, Rufus S. "Distribution of Tax Burdens in 1948." NATIONAL TAX JOURNAL, 4 (Sept. 1951), 269-285.

U.S. Congress Senate. Committee on Labor and Public Welfare. MANPOWER DEVELOPMENT AND TRAINING LEGISLATION, 1970. Hearings before the Subcommittee on Employment, Manpower, and Poverty, on S.3867, S.2838, S.3878. 91st Congs., 1st and 2d sess. Washington, D.C.: Government Printing Office, 1970.

U.S. Department of Labor. MANPOWER REPORT OF THE PRESIDENT. Washington, D.C.: Government Printing Office, March, 1970.

U.S. Internal Revenue Service. STATISTICS OF INCOME 1967: INDIVIDUAL INCOME TAX RETURNS. Washington, D.C.: Government Printing Office, 1969.

U.S. Manpower Administration. REQUEST FOR PROPOSAL MA-3. Washington, D.C.: Government Printing Office, 1968.

U.S. Office of Manpower Policy, Evaluation and Research. ECONOMIC BENEFITS AND COSTS OF RETRAINING COURSES IN MICHIGAN. By Micheal E. Borus and Einar Hardin. Washington, D.C.: Government Printing Office, 1969.

Index

Index

Absenteeism, xvi, xvii, 13, 23, 24, 36, 39, 80; in theory of human capital, 6-8; and adjustments within firm, 8; and subsidized training, 38; in multivariate analysis, 40; impact of OJT upon, 46-47; in shipbuilding company program, 53-55, 58, 61; in electronic components manufacturing program, 69, 72, 74

Administrators, manpower program, 81-82

Age, 51-52, 55, 79; and hiring criteria, 38, 43, 69; in comparison between subsidized trainees and control group, 45; and MA-3 program, 47

Aggregate demand, 80; expansion of, 82-83

Applicants, job, 9-10, 11, 23; matched to vacancies, xiii. *See also* Hiring

ARA, 31

Attendance rate, *see* Absenteeism

Attitudes, firm's, xvii

Becker, Gary, 1

Benefits: distribution of, xiv-xvii, 24, 35; and shareholders, 14, 16-17; and tied subsidies, 19-21; to trainees, 19, 29-30, 57-58, 75-77, 79, 82; in shipbuilding company program, 57-58; in electronic components manufacturer's program, 74-76; to disadvantaged, 79, 82

Benton Harbor, Michigan, 33

Borus, Michael E., 27, 29-34 *passim*

Capital, human, xv, 1-24; and theory of the firm, 2-9; investment approach, 2-3; cost parameters, 3; and screening and recruitment, 3; and productivity, 4-6; and absenteeism, 6-8; and turnover, 8-10; and heterogeneous population of job applicants, 9-10 implications for manpower programs, 11-12; and manpower program output distribution, 12-23

Characteristics, socioeconomic, 35, 38-41, 43; trainee-control group comparisons, 43-47, 67-69, 72, 76; of fast and slow learners, 55-56; and absenteeism, 72; and hiring practices, 81

Concentrated Employment Program, 38

Consumer, xiii, 35

Cost-benefit studies, 27-41; Borus Hardin, 29-33; author's methodology, 34-41; multivariate analysis, 40, 46-47; regres-

sion models, 47-48; multicollinearity, 48-49

Costs: distribution of, xiv-xv; and tied subsidies, 19; impact of OJT on, 46-47; of vestibule training, 59-60, 74-75

Counseling, xiv

Detroit, 33

Disadvantaged, xiii, xvi-xvii, 23-24; income and consumption, 1; and wage subsidy, 16; and firm's risk aversion, 17; benefits to, 79; and tightening of labor market, 82

Distribution effects, 35, 75, 77, 80, 82

Doeringer, Peter, 11

Earnings, *see* Income; Wages

Education, 40, 45, 55, 82; and hiring criteria, 39, 43, 52; and job performance measures, 69; and labor market, 79

Efficiency, 36, 80; economic, xvii; in training, 5-6; and vestibule training, 74-75

Electronic components manufacturer, 37, 67-77, 79; and wage and job assignment practices, 37-38; trainee-control group comparisons of socioeconomic characteristics, 67-69; multivariate analysis, 69-73; turnover, 69-71; absenteeism, 72, 74; productivity, 72-73, 80; program benefits, 74-77; benefits to firm, 74-75, 80; benefits to employees, 75-76, 77, 79; program efficiency, 80

Employment, 29, 69; opportunities, xiii, 34; full, 11; generated by wage subsidy, 14-15; generated by training programs, 29

Employer, xiv, xv

Experience, 50, 69; and turnover rate, 51

Flint, Michigan, 33

Funding, xiii-xiv

Hardin, Einar, 27, 30-34 *passim*

Hiring, xv, xvi, xvii, 57; impact of manpower program on, 1, 79, 81; and theory of the firm, 2-3; under wage subsidy, 12-13; criteria, 38-39, 40-41, 43; trainee-control group comparisons, 43-46, 67, 69; alteration of criteria, 81-82

Income, xiii; and manpower programs, 11-12, 27-28; and subsidized training

95

97

Taxpayer, xv, 28, 80; and wage subsidy,
14, 16; and training subsidy, 23; in
evaluation of project's social value, 35,
36
Trainees, 19; cost-benefit studies of,
28-34; in author's study design, 35, 37;
socioeconomic characteristics, 35;
selection, 36; benefits to, and shipbuilding company program, 64; benefits to in electronic components manufacturer's program, 75-76
Training, xiii-xvi; cost of, xvii, 24, 35-36,
74, 75; impact of manpower program,
1; and theory of the firm, 3-4, 24; and
productivity, 4-6; and absenteeism,
6-8; and turnover, 8-9; and job-appli-
cant population, 9-10; subsidy, 18-23;
benefits from tying subsidies to, 19-22;
firms that would seek subsidies, 22-23
Training program: selection of, 5; efficiency of, 5-6; West Virginia, 29; social
value of, 29; length of, 31-34; benefits
for shipbuilder, 57-58; and electronic
components manufacturer, 70, 72
Turnover, xvi, xvii, 2, 13, 23, 24, 36, 38,
39, 80; in theory of human capital, 8-9;
and wage structure, 20; impact of sub-

sidized OJT on, 46-47; and shipbuilding company program, 48-53, 58, 60,
61; correlation with previous experience, 50-52; correlation with unemployment, 52; in electronic components manufacturing company, 69-71,
74; impact of vestibule training on, 70,
74; and cost of training, 74, 75

Unemployment, 11, 30, 68, 70, 79; and
turnover, 52; generation of, 76

Vacancies, job, matching applicant to, xiii

Wages, xvi, xvii, 23; impact of manpower
programs on, 1; and benefits of general
training, 4-5; and implications of
human capital model, 11; subsidization
of, 12-18; subsidies tied to training,
19-20, 29-30, 34; and shipbuilding
company program, 37, 50, 52, 58,
63-64; and electronic components
manufacturer, 76
Wage theory, 2-3
West Virginia, 29
World War II, 82

About the Author

Corry F. Azzi received the Ph.D. in economics from Harvard University in February, 1972. He is currently assistant professor of economics at Lawrence University, Appleton, Wisconsin.

Since receipt of his degree, Dr. Azzi has published papers in the *Quarterly Journal of Economics* on public expenditure theory. This book is the result of his interest in public tax-expenditure theory and applied work in public policy.